One More Day

THE JOE CHRISTENSEN STORY

Joe Christensen

One More Day
The Joe Christensen Story

Authored by Joe Christensen
Edited by Ann Del Ponte and Sarah Derozier

Cover design by Travis Vanden Heuvel.
Cover photo © Tyler Gajewski (used with permission).

*Every reasonable effort has been made to cite sources and
determine copyright holders of the material in this book
and to secure permissions needed. If any citations have been
inadvertently omitted or copyrighted materials have been
inadvertently included in this book without the proper credit
being given in one form or another, please contact Peregrino
Press in writing so that any future printings of this book may
be corrected accordingly.*

ISBN: 978-0-9969426-6-9

a Peregrino Press book

De Pere, Wisconsin

DEDICATION

*Blessed are they who are persecuted for the sake of
righteousness, for theirs is the kingdom of heaven.*
— Matthew 5:10

This book is dedicated to everyone on the margins.
If you've ever felt alone or afraid, tired or troubled, if you've
ever been bullied or put down, laughed at or poked fun of,
know that you don't journey alone…and that I will always
have your back.

With love,
JC

CONTENTS

THANKS FROM THE AUTHOR

As I wrote this book - chapter by chapter and word for word - I thought of every single person that helped make his project possible. There was never one single person that supported this project. Every person I know supported me. For that, I am very thankful and proud to know that everyone always had my back. No negatives were ever involved. Each positive made this bigger and better, not only as a book, but it also made me grow and become that much better as a person. I smiled every step of the way, always realizing that my dream was on its way to becoming a reality. I never thought I would have the ability or passion to write my life story in book form. However, knowing I had the right supportive crew helping me achieve a dream of mine, it made it that much easier to accomplish.

First off, I would like to thank my friends. The many of you should know who you are, whether we are near or far. You may not realize this, but as I relived this story - my life - I thought of each and every one of you. To my friends from Kennedy, you will always hold a special spot in my heart and mind. From understanding who Joey the person was to taking me to your house or sitting at the same lunch table with me, you all made my schooling experience that much easier. There were a lot of unknowns, yes, but because of you, I made it through. I was challenged here and there, but not one of you cared about how I looked, walked, or used only one side of my body. You spoke to me like you would any other person at that school. I smiled knowing all of this and felt like one of them. One of the students. You all embraced me rather that ignoring me. My heart beamed with joy because of that. I know that a lot of us didn't see each other during the school day, but odds are, I watched your actions and knew because of the positivity within your hearts and mind, to you, I was just like everyone else you talked to. You respected me. For all of the acceptance and love each and every one of you gave me, thank you.

To those who saw me struggle in my middle school years, thank you for being supportive down that road that started out very dark but became light and bright. I had not known the majority of you when I came to Pulaski and considered myself a loner, but as each passing day went on, it got easier. It got easier knowing that you accepted me for me. You made me have more courage and strength to know that it was going to take time to adjust, but it would get better. Every single class had different situations involved. Some more challenging than others. But once I got to know you and you got to know me, it got that much easier to evolve to everything and everyone around you. Whether I talked to you during class, outside of school, or even got to know you on a more person level, thank you for making the journey easier and less stressful. It wasn't easy, by far, but with the positive attitudes and the remarkable acceptance you had with and for me, I got through it with pride. Even though I had a pretty close knit group of friends at Kennedy, I will forever be thankful for you all being my new friends away from home. Thank you for being so kind.

To the myTEAM TRIUMPH organization: You've opened up new and exciting roads for someone who never thought he would be able to walk through. From the executive director, to the staff, all the way to the Angels I've had the awesome pleasure of teaming up with, I cannot thank you enough. There will never be enough words I can say for how thankful I am to be a part of this family. I consider you all my second family, since the first day I started with mTT. It all started as a trial run to see if I would actually like doing what you do for those who are differently abled, to now being Captain Ambassador for the organization. I never ever thought I would accomplish as much as I have with you all. You build real life authentic relationships with everyone involved, and I love that. I cannot fathom how accepting you would be of me, because I was entering unknown territory. I tried something new, that I've never done before, and am happier every day because of that. Each race I've participated in I have smile from the starting line all the way to saying goodbye to my teammates after the race. I started in 2012 and here it is 2017 and I am still going strong. That right there, is because of mTT and everyone I race or raced with, talked to, crossed the finish line with, or even helped form sponsorships with. I am even doing my first ever full marathon this year because of the acceptance, growth and love I have received from mTT. I will forever love each and every single one of you for making my life that much better. Thank you all from the bottom of my heart.

Lastly comes my family. First off my parents. I was a heck of a surprise and shouldn't even be typing this, but it was because of your strength and believing in me from the moment I was born that I am here. I gave you both quite the fight to put up with, having more good days than bad days, but not a moment goes by that I don't thank you and know that you love me for who I am and what I've done to make you proud. Thank you for being my parents. I love you.

Then comes the siblings. Although I will always have some type of struggle every day, I love how you each check in on me even in the smallest of ways. Your protective covering for me is something I will forever cherish, no matter how stubborn I may be. Knowing you are only looking out for me and wanting me to make the best out of life is something I'll always remember. I love you all.

To my aunts and uncle: Thank you for always making me smile. I may not see you every day, but always remember that I know you do care now and will until my end of this life. From our fishing adventures to surgeries and hospital stays, I love you.

To the many, many cousins that I have: You each have your own way of making me smile. From our shopping adventures to our one on one talks, my smile grows because of all of you. Love you all.

To my stepfather: We started out as strangers. But knowing you look at me just like another simple, easygoing person who can make you laugh and smile at the same time, makes my heart fonder of the relationship we've formed. Your support through both my good days and bad will always be with me. I know you respect me so always remember, I will respect you.

The very last thanks I would like to give out is to Grandma. You've always had a nickname for me, Joe Joe. Truth be told, you are not only the rock of the family but also are the one person who I know will always find a way to make me smile, even on a bad day-you have done that numerous times. I know that you will always worry about me and for that, I thank you. From our daily visits to our phone conversations, always know that because of things like those, I smile. Thank you, Grandma, for being so loving and supportive of me each and every day. I love you.

A NOTE FROM THE PUBLISHER

Courage is not something that you already have that makes you brave when the tough times start. Courage is what you earn when you've been through the tough times and you discover they aren't so tough after all.

— *Malcolm Gladwell*

As I WRITE THIS, we find ourselves closing in on Easter Sunday, 2017. And while my family's journey this Lent has been familiar, my wife and I are navigating new terrain. Jess and I have been blessed with an incredibly intelligent–and insatiably inquisitive–daughter who is now old enough, and curious enough, to be asking questions about Jesus. "Why was Jesus arrested?" "Why didn't the priests like Him?" "Why didn't anyone stop them from hurting Jesus?" What we find striking, though, aren't the questions that she asks, but rather the ones she doesn't.

Faith, now almost 5 years old, isn't asking about Jesus' death and resurrection. When we explain that Jesus had to die because He loves us, because He wanted to save us, she's surprisingly satisfied with that fact. What gives her trouble, and peeks her interest, is how people acted and reacted, or failed to act altogether, toward the Son of God. This provides us as parents with a great opportunity, a teachable moment. "How should we treat others?" we'll ask. "Would you help someone if they were in trouble?"

How fitting, then, that at the same time my family is preparing for Holy Week, Peregrino Press is preparing to launch this book. *One More Day: The Joe Christensen Story* has us reflect on the ways in which we can, in our everyday lives, share joy and love and grace and faith with one another. After reading this book, when confronted with a problem or challenge, I'm confident you'll find yourself asking, "WWJD?" "What would Joey do?"

This Easter season, with Joe's journey fresh on my mind, I can't help but recognize the similarities between my two friends who share the same initials: JC, Jesus Christ and Joey Christensen. Both came into this world as beautiful, innocent baby boys; both of them born to die, but given the strength and spirit to conquer death in their own unique way; both of them on a mission to fight evil and inequality while also being beacons of light and hope. And both of them sent to save the world ... one parable, one presentation, at a time.

Just as the life of Christ continues to inspire us today, Joe's work, his example, and his influence will have an impact on people for years to come. Most of us are familiar with *The Butterfly Effect;* the concept that a cyclone in India can be the result of a butterfly flapping its wings in

Wisconsin. Small actions, performed at the perfect time, in the perfect space, can have a big impact. For those of you who know Joe, you know how big of an impact he's already had on so many.

In 1969, American philosopher and educator Loren Eiseley penned an essay titled, "The Starfish Thrower." The story has been adapted and changed over the years, but the moral has remained the same: What we do in life matters.

> There was an older man walking along the shore, picking up starfish and throwing them out into the water. A young boy, having watched the man for some time, ran up to him asking, "What are you doing?" A bit startled, the man replied, "These starfish have been washed ashore with the tide. If they stay here on the beach, in the hot morning sun, they will shrivel up and die." The boy, more curious now than before, said, "But there are millions of starfish on this beach. And just this one beach goes on for miles. How do you expect to make any difference at all?" The old man smiled, bent down, picked up a starfish, and threw it as far as he could into the safety of the sea. "I made a difference to that one."

We may never know the full impact that Joe has had on this world or how many lives he's changed. But I know he's made a difference in the life of at least one person... my life has been forever changed because of him. And after reading this book, I suspect that you, too, will develop a newfound appreciation for life and the gifts you've been given.

***

Throughout his professional life, Joe has been traveling across Wisconsin and the Midwest speaking to schools and businesses about the importance of treating people with dignity and respect. The central theme of his presentation is bullying, but, just like his path through life, Joe's approach to this subject is anything but conventional. His message focuses on the power of positive thinking, so it's appropriate that he takes on the issue of bullying not as a problem, but as an opportunity.

Over the years, unsuspecting audiences have filled auditoriums and gymnasiums to hear Joe speak. Often times, the only information they have about him is that he is physically disabled and that he's on a mission to end bullying in schools and workplaces. It's regularly assumed that Joe will tell those gathered about the negative impact that bullies had on him growing up and being different. Instead, Joe dedicates his time to introducing his audiences to different men and women, boys and girls, who went out of their way to befriend him. Joe points to these friends as the sources of his own joy, hope, and optimism. If you've seen Joe speak, you understand just how impactful this is.

In the context of bulling, we tend to focus on the *don't*s. Don't point. Don't stare. Don't use hurtful words. Being the eternal optimist that he is, Joe challenges us to redirect our energy. Instead of *not* acting like a bully, he calls us to imitate the compassion of a friend. Subtle, yet powerful, the examples Joe gives of people going out of their way to treat him like they would anyone else call all of us to action. After hearing about the experiences that have shaped his life, we can't help but be inspired to reciprocate kindness and grace–the same kind that was extended to Joe–to people in our own lives.

How would our lives be different if we recognized that everyone has inherent value and worth? Joe uses his life as a testament to what our world should and could look like if we lived by *The Golden Rule*.

***

To give you some background on how this project came to fruition, it's important to share with you the genesis and mission of Peregrino Press. The story begins with a heart attack in 1993. Fr. John Tourangeau, a Norbertine priest of De Pere, WI, then serving in the Diocese of Santa Fe, NM, was celebrating Mass when he went into cardiac arrest. He would go on to have a near-death experience (NDE) on the operating room table, venture to the threshold of heaven, have a conversation with Jesus, and come back to life here on earth. Two decades would pass before Fr. John would begin speaking publicly about his NDE.

Later, after a few years of telling his story–a presentation titled "Heaven: Is it for real?"–to over 10,000 people around the country, Fr. John was approached by a major publishing company and offered a book deal. Excited to share his story with a wider audience, Father jumped at the chance to tell his tale in book form. But after a series of incidents where the publisher insisted on taking "artistic liberties" with his story (embellishing it in an attempt to sell more books), Fr. John walked away from the project. Sensationalizing the events of his life in the interest of becoming a bestselling author wasn't what he sought to do. If published, his story needed to be true. It needed to be authentic.

At the same time, Fr. John was serving as pastor at St. Norbert College Parish in De Pere, where my family and I are parishioners. John had become a close friend over the years, and I was following his presentations and upcoming book deal closely. When he told me that he was no longer writing a book, I was saddened. When he told me the reason he was no longer writing a book, I was upset. "What do you need them (the publisher) for?! I can help you!" I exclaimed. (*Mind you, my language was a bit more colorful in person; illustrating not only how frustrated I was with the situation, but also the close relationship that Father and I share.*) "Let's start our own publishing company and get your story out there!" Little did I know what God had in store for us.

In late summer, 2015, Fr. John and I published *To Heaven & Back: The Journey of a Roman Catholic Priest* — now a #1 Amazon Bestseller — and co-founded Peregrino Press. Although our mission at the time was to give voice to Fr. John's words, we found that Father's experience with a large publishing house wasn't unique. Larger publishers, taking books to market the traditional way, tend to have a singular focus, selling books. This is a priority that can easily compete with, and often overshadow, an author's desire to tell an authentic story. It became our mission to provide authors a platform to share *their* stories without a filter or the need for dramatization.

Joe Christiansen and I have been friends since elementary school. When I saw the work that he was doing in our community, and married that up with our mission of authentic storytelling, Peregrino Press jumped at the opportunity to offer Joe a book deal. As you'll see in the pages to come, we paid special attention to ensuring that

Joe kept his voice throughout the entire book. *One More Day* is a story about Joe, by Joe. Real. Authentic. Perfectly imperfect.

Enjoy!

Travis J. Vanden Heuvel
president & publisher
Peregrino Press

FOREWORD

"Sometimes it is the people no one can imagine any-thing of who do the things no one can imagine."

— *Alan Turing*

WHAT PRAISE CAN COME from your pain?

Joe came into my life when he became involved as a Captain and Ambassador of our mission at myTEAM TRIUMPH. Immediately after connecting, I could tell that Joe was different. What did I see that was different? The unique way he walks? The challenges he has with hearing? The way he struggles to do every day things with basically one functional arm? No! What I saw different about Joe was his perspective!

No one can deny the struggle that Joe and his family have faced as they dealt with the roadblocks of disability.

However, Joe and his family have not seen these as road-blocks but rather as detours on the road of significance.

Let's face it, the world looks at challenges as things we need to avoid. We are programmed to go through life on the path of least resistance. We eliminate challenging people, avoid new experiences, hide from anything that makes us grow. Joe lives his life with a grateful perspective. What if we could choose the attitude that sees challenges as unexpected blessings?

Are you ready for a shift in thinking? Are you prepared to have a move of feeling, thought, and spirit? Put you shoulder pads on, lace up your shoes, and get ready to grow! Joe's story will help you see your setbacks as set ups to something greater in your life.

Christen Jensen
Executive Director
myTEAM TRIUMPH., WI

INTRODUCTION

The Lord is my light and my salvation—
whom shall I fear?
The Lord is the stronghold of my life—
of whom shall I be afraid?

Psalm 27:1

BEING ALIVE TODAY IS a gift, yet most people take it for granted. Looking at life and asking, "Why are we here and what is my purpose in this life?" are not questions people commonly ask themselves. Throughout this book, you'll read about my personal journey from the good, to the not-so-good, to everything in between. Throughout my life, I have been taught that there is something bigger and better for every single one of us, regardless of our given situation, which I believe is our God-given situation.

It is my belief that we, as humans, should and will be challenged in life. These challenges will be both physical and mental, but we always have the encouragement of our peers and the knowledge that we are loved by everyone around us. Defying the odds and being alive today is a gift that I have never taken for granted. The way I choose to live my life is my gift back to my Creator.

I can't deny it has been an interesting journey for me thus far. Giving up on myself or on God has never been an option, as I feel there is a reason and purpose for my existence. My hope is that all people will look deep inside their hearts and one day recognize there is a reason they received the gift of life.

I share my story with everyone around me. From the tears to the smiles, the struggles to the triumphs, I will forever wear a smile. Good or bad, it's all part of the story. I may not have the ability to use one side of my body, and I live with multiple everyday battles, but guess what? That is OK.

People are not built the exact same way, and your life's situations and personal battles should never stop you from living life to its fullest potential. I am not disabled—I am differently abled.

My sincere hope as you read this book is that you realize your story is powerful. Your story has meaning. But in order for anyone to hear it, it needs to be shared. That's how your story has meaning to not only you, but to those around you. It's up to you to figure out how to do things in life. Just remember, all things are possible. It's your story, so make it an impactful one.

People are often unreasonable, irrational, and self-centered. Forgive them, anyway.

If you are kind, people may accuse you of selfish, ulterior motives. Be kind, anyway.

If you are successful, you will win some unfaithful friends and some genuine enemies. Succeed, anyway.

If you are honest and sincere people may deceive you. Be honest and sincere, anyway.

What you spend years creating, others could destroy overnight. Create, anyway.

If you find serenity and happiness, some may be jealous. Be happy, anyway.

The good you do today will often be forgotten. Do good, anyway.

Give the best you have, and it will never be enough. Give your best, anyway.

In the final analysis, it is between you and God. It was never between you and them, anyway.

— Mother Teresa

CHAPTER ONE: DIFFERENTLY-ABLED

All the adversity I've had in my life, all my troubles and obstacles, have strengthened me.... You may not realize it when it happens, but a kick in the teeth may be the best thing in the world for you.

—Walt Disney

IMAGINE, IF YOU WILL, a world free of judgment and stereotypes. What would that look like to you? How would it make you feel? Would you go to a store, a concert, your school, or even just be outdoors and change how you value someone based on how they look on the outside? Would you be interested in learning what is inside a person before determining his or her worth?

Are you seeing an amazing world when you envision this? Not knowing what is inside of a person by seeing a fraction and making judgments and opinions would change dramatically. If we begin to learn what a person is both inside and out, we will begin to seek quality and purpose in the relationships and contact we have with one another. What a beautiful concept!

The most common word I hear in reference to myself and others like me is "disabled." Words associated with disabled range from crippled, to disadvantaged, to invalid. Those of us labeled "handicapped" are certainly not any of those negative terms. We are ABLED differently. To me, the correct word is neither disabled nor handicapped. Rather, the term that I've learned and come to embrace is "differently abled." We are capable and abled, we just do daily tasks in a different way. Yes, it will probably take us longer to do each task than others, but we can do it.

If you sit back and think about it, everyone is differently abled in some way, shape, or form. For me, it is and will always be in the form of the physical. For those who are not differently abled physically are differently abled in other ways. It could relate to the reliance of daily medication, a mental condition, or even just a habit. It's figuring out you can do the things you never thought you could until you tried—a uniqueness. Whatever it may be, we need to be accepting and encouraging toward one another; not causing the feeling of being unwanted or unloved because of different abilities. It is a part of what makes you, you. We must embrace ourselves rather than feel sorry for ourselves. Accept the life you've been given. It's a good one if you let it be!

People who are differently abled physically still lead extraordinary lives. The bigger things like marriage, children, work, and a growing extended family are important. The smaller things such as participating in sports, marathons, or spending time on a hobby have meaning. For some, being differently abled physically requires the use of a wheel-chair. Yet, those individuals can still fish, hunt, and even drive. Being differently abled physically doesn't hold them back from being part of something amazing.

Realistically, those of us who are differently abled physically are far more capable than others realize. It fact, it's what keeps us from being ordinary. No one is exactly the same. We are not meant to be. That is the beauty of life, which I've come to know very well. I may look and do things a little differently, but I am human… just like you!

I've seen and heard how some people react upon meeting me, or others similar to me. The reaction is often pity, which includes thoughts of "this poor person" or "oh, my gosh how awful." But we don't want others feeling sorry for us. Many who are differently abled physically don't think of themselves as being any different than those who are able bodied. We live with a few curves in life that, at times, can be difficult but we take great pride in overcoming them.

Our challenges in life will always change us. Being differently abled physically is something we take to heart and are extremely proud of. Some might think we will eventually crawl up in a ball and give up. That is not, nor will it ever be, an option. We were given this life with these predicaments for a reason. That's why I have chosen to show my gratitude and thank God for the life I was given.

The next time you see people who are "handicapped," don't immediately judge them based on outward appearance. Walk up to them and say hello. Find out their abilities and learn how they define themselves. Don't treat them differently. Treat us all with respect and dignity and, without a doubt, you'll get that right back from us.

THINK | PRAY | MEDITATE

Our deepest fear is not that we are inadequate. Our deepest fear is that we are powerful beyond measure. It is our light, not our darkness that most frightens us. We ask ourselves, 'Who am I to be brilliant, gorgeous, talented, fabulous?' Actually, who are you not to be? You are a child of God. Your playing small does not serve the world. There is nothing enlightened about shrinking so that other people won't feel insecure around you. We are all meant to shine, as children do. We were born to make manifest the glory of God that is within us. It's not just in some of us; it's in everyone. And as we let our own light shine, we unconsciously give other people permission to do the same. As we are liberated from our own fear, our presence automatically liberates others.

— Marianne Williamson

CHAPTER TWO: MY BIRTH STORY

And there were shepherds living out in the fields nearby,
keeping watch over their flocks at night. An angel of
the Lord appeared to them, and the glory of the Lord
shone around them, and they were terrified. But the
angel said to them, "Do not be afraid. I bring you good
news that will cause great joy for all the people. Today
in the town of David a Savior has been born to you;
he is the Messiah, the Lord. This will be a sign to you:
You will find a baby wrapped in cloths and lying in a
manger."

Luke 2:8-12

IT SEEMS TO ME there are two types of people in this world
who face adversities of all kinds, whether they be physical
or mental. One type rises up to overcome the challenges

they've been given. The other type allows adversities to consume them, becoming bitter and negative. I was given quite the unfortunate start in life, but I chose to not let that define me as a whole. God gave me His hand in strength as well as the ability to spread His love.

The rough start I endured in my earliest of days made me feel that God blessed me with a journey like no other. Personally, being born was a test—a test to see if I would trust Him. With Him by my side, I took that test and forcefully took it to victory. I should not be alive, which is why I believe both God and I have big plans to spread His word and love.

As humans, we all face the unknown, which starts with when we will be born. Not every plan goes as smoothly as we hope. Odds are there will be bumps and setbacks, little learning curves. Truth be told, that is the entire purpose. No one's journey into this world is the same. God wants us to succeed, yet sometimes He hands us challenges as soon as we are born. These struggles early on in life allow us to show Him how thankful we are for this life.

My entrance into this world was far from easy. My birth on that March day was unexpected by everyone involved. Tears were shed. Many questions were, and still are, asked to medical professionals. Why did this happen? What could have been done differently to avoid this heartbreaking ordeal? Was this how it was meant to be? In God's mind—yes. Every tear, every heart-sinking moment was a way of letting my family know that it was going to be a struggle. God wanted them to know I was a fighter.

At some point in our lives, we get thrown all out of sorts. It's a test given by Him. He wants those struggles to be turned into triumphs. It may not be today, or tomorrow, but someday. He will ask for your trust to let Him know you are here for a reason. You have purpose. You survived. He created us all as a mold from His vision. It is His hope that we use that purpose and show it not only to ourselves and to Him, but to those around us.

So what are you going to do? Are you going to give up? Or are you going to keep going and prove your capabilities to yourself and to Him? The choice is yours.

The Angelus

The Angel of the Lord declared to Mary:

And she conceived of the Holy Spirit.

> Hail Mary, full of grace, the Lord is with thee; blessed art thou among women and blessed is the fruit of thy womb, Jesus. Holy Mary, Mother of God, pray for us sinners, now and at the hour of our death. Amen.

Behold the handmaid of the Lord: Be it done unto me according to Thy word.

Hail Mary...

And the Word was made Flesh: And dwelt among us.

Hail Mary...

Pray for us, O Holy Mother of God, that we may be made worthy of the promises of Christ.

Let us pray:

Pour forth, we beseech Thee, O Lord, Thy grace into our hearts; that we, to whom the incarnation of Christ, Thy Son, was made known by the message of an angel, may by His Passion and Cross be brought to the glory of His Resurrection, through the same Christ Our Lord. Amen.

CHAPTER THREE: THE

FIRST TEST OF LIFE

For I am convinced that neither death nor life, neither angels nor demons, neither the present nor the future, nor any powers, neither height nor depth, nor anything else in all creation, will be able to separate us from the love of God that is in Christ Jesus our Lord.

Romans 8:38-39

M Y MOM DEE WENT to the bowling alley the evening of March 3 feeling fine. When it was her turn to bowl, she stepped up to the lane and threw a ball. She remembers feeling a crushing pain that caused her to double over. She almost couldn't stand up.

My dad Don had come to the bowling alley with my

two sisters, Jenny and Melissa, to watch my mom bowl. They ended up going home early because my mother's pain was not subsiding. My grandmother and two aunts came to our home to take care of my sisters, and my parents went to the hospital. My mother never saw a doctor that night. She was told it was gas and they recommended over-the-counter medication to help with the pain. They also encouraged her to walk as much as possible. Standing up straight for my mom was nearly impossible due to the pain; still, she was released from the hospital that night.

When she got home, she took the meds and walked continuously, but the pain wasn't going away. It was getting progressively worse. My parents called the hospital back only to be told my mother should take more medication. It was getting late and the rest of the family was going to bed, but all my mother was physically able to do was walk. She tried lying down, only to get shooting pains. She just continued to walk through the night.

My aunt Debbie came over the following morning while my mom was making beds. My upset aunt asked her what she was doing. She replied that it felt better if she kept moving. They called the doctor's office again and this time went right over. The doctor informed my mom that she could have a bladder infection (but she was in so much pain she couldn't provide a urine sample), she could be in labor, or "we won't discuss the third possibility."

My mom was shuttled immediately to the Emergency Room. She was told to go to the fourth floor because she couldn't go to the maternity ward since she wasn't in labor. After she arrived on the fourth floor, she put on a hospital gown but was still in severe pain. A nurse came in, asked her why she was on this floor, and sent her to the maternity floor. So, in a wheelchair, she was taken to the maternity floor and was put her in a room. Now getting shooting pain up through her shoulder, she proceeded to ask a nurse what was causing it. The nurse gave her a vague answer of, "I don't know." My mom told the nurse that she was supposed to have an ultrasound. But the nurse told her there was no order for one. A few minutes later, the nurse returned to tell her she was right and indeed needed an ultrasound. My mother remembers a nurse looking at the screen of the ultrasound machine and poking the nurse next to her. She had three doctors at her side in a matter of minutes.

My mother later described feeling a sensation that the walls were spinning and that's when the doctor slapped her cheek and told her they had no choice but to do an emergency cesarean section. The doctors and nurses couldn't see a baby on the ultrasound. At this point, my mother just wanted it to be over as the pain was horrendous. They did a cesarean section immediately.

The third of four children, I, Joseph Donald Christensen, was born at 12:24 p.m. on the 4th of March in 1986. My mother woke up shortly after 2 p.m. in the recovery room. Aunt Debbie was with her in the room, but I was rushed to a Neonatal Intensive Care Unit in another hospital. No one thought I would make it through the night. My life was so fragile that I was immediately baptized by a priest. I was born 10 weeks early, weighing only 3 pounds and 14 ounces. My mother told my aunt she wanted to name me after my great-grandfather Joseph, who was an amazing, strong, and loving man.

I was stable for a couple hours following my birth, but then both of my lungs collapsed. I developed a grade 4 brain bleed on the right side of my brain, which controls the left side of my body. The bleed healed on its own just before doctors were set to operate to insert a shunt.

My mother was put in her hospital room where doctors and nurses removed the IV from her arm. Shortly after removing the IV, they came back to her room and informed her she needed three units of blood, so another IV was put in. They didn't realize she was bleeding internally all night because of a ruptured uterus.

That would make not only one error, but two, as she was misdiagnosed with gas pains the night before. The doctor who misdiagnosed my mom over the phone stood at her door, never stepping foot inside the hospital room. The only thing he said to her was, "Good thing you were so persistent or we'd be visiting you and your son at Schauer and Schumacher Funeral Home." She then called my grandma, crying.

She was the mother of a newborn but had yet to see her baby. No family member had seen me. But I was busy putting up quite a fight in another hospital. Thank the good Lord my mother could call the NICU at that hospital from her room at another hospital whenever she wanted to check on me. My medical team kept her informed of my condition, whether it be good or bad news. She received news of improvement but she also heard about some setbacks.

Complications from birth, the pneumothorax, and a dropping heart rate meant I needed chest tubes. The medical team inserted one chest tube, then another, and continued until five tubes were in place.

I was placed on a respirator, which I continually fought, so the doctors decided to keep me sedated. It wasn't until I was three days old that my mother was able to meet me. The medical team told her to be prepared, as I had a lot of tubes and machines attached to my body. My mother met all of my doctors, many of whom I still have today. The doctors gave my parents a lot of information and explanations. The next morning, she was released from the hospital, but would be going home without her newborn baby. She left with only balloons, cards, and gifts to return home to her two daughters, ages 6 and 4.

Meanwhile, a team of nurses at the hospital across town stayed by my side 24 hours a day, seven days a week. I was in the center of the room where the sickest of babies were placed because they required the most care. My lungs were stiff due to the lack of a chemical called surfactant. Care was needed every minute of every day.

When visiting me in the hospital, many family members were shocked by my appearance. My tiny body was covered with tubes, which were held down by tape and connected to machines to ensure my body functioned correctly. The lights and beeping sounds kept the nurses, doctors, and my family apprised of my condition. I could only be touched through an incubator, but my mother tried to comfort me the best she could. A lot of tears were shed.

Many people told my parents to consult a lawyer. The records from the hospital where I was born would be needed. When my mother went to pick up the files, there was no record of her ever having been a patient there. The lawyer my parents met with told them it would be a hard fight going against a doctor. My parents decided to leave the situation as it was. They didn't have the financial ability to pursue a legal journey.

My parents eventually sat down with the doctor who treated my mother and confronted him. They wanted to know what the hell had happened. The doctor informed them he had learned about my mother's condition in medical school, but he hadn't heard of anyone surviving it. My mother's uterus had ruptured, leaving a hole the size of a golf ball. The tear was large enough for a baby to go through. He was convinced walking all night is what saved both of our lives, but was unsure as to how. With that, he gave my parents a piece of vital information: both my mother and I should have bled to death. There is no medical reason for her or me to be alive. By the grace of God and His healing hands, we are still here.

So, the medical journey continued with my parents making multiple trips to the hospital every day. My sisters were allowed into the NICU to see their newborn brother, but they didn't understand how ill I was. When they came for a visit, the nurses gave them gowns to wear and let them sit behind the nurse's station with coloring books and crayons.

Two weeks after my birth, my mom went back to where it all began, Ashwaubenon Bowling Alley. She saw her bowling teammates and several of her friends. Unfortunately, the laughs and smiles didn't last long. She returned home to my dad, who was upset. He told her the hospital called to report I had developed pneumonia. Again, no one thought I would make it through the night. Again, I proved them wrong.

On Mom's birthday, the 6th of April, I came off of the respirator. When my mom went to see me, she was greeted by rounds of applause from the NICU nurses. It was a birthday present she would never forget. I would end up spending 88 days in the NICU.

THINK | PRAY | MEDITATE

Paul's Prayer for Spiritual Growth

When I think of all this, I fall to my knees and pray to the Father, the Creator of everything in heaven and on earth. I pray that from his glorious, unlimited resources he will empower you with inner strength through his Spirit. Then Christ will make his home in your hearts as you trust in him. Your roots will grow down into God's love and keep you strong. And may you have the power to understand, as all God's people should, how wide, how long, how high, and how deep his love is. May you experience the love of Christ, though it is too great to understand fully. Then you will be made complete with all the fullness of life and power that comes from God.

Now all glory to God, who is able, through his mighty power at work within us, to accomplish infinitely more than we might ask or think. Glory to him in the church and in Christ Jesus through all generations forever and ever! Amen.

Ephesians 3:14-21

CHAPTER FOUR: LET

SCHOOLING BEGIN

Start children off on the way they should go, and even when they are old they will not turn from it.

Proverbs 22:6

S TARTING SCHOOL AND ITS adventures can be very pleasing. It can nurture your soul, preparing you as a whole person. Imagine yourself—shiny new shoes, a freshly packed lunch, and a big backpack to show off to your new friends and teachers—stepping onto a shiny new floor in your home away from home. Nothing but good things can happen from here on, right?

Technically, my first learning experience was at the CP Center in Green Bay where I started therapy when I was just 3 months old and where I eventually learned to walk at age 4.

I was diagnosed with Cerebral Palsy—hemiplegia to be precise—as a newborn when I was still in the hospital. The condition affects one side of the body, including the arm, leg, and trunk. In my case, it affects my left side. I also have significant hearing loss, which I'll discuss in an upcoming chapter.

I rode a school bus and went to a regular school from kindergarten through graduation from high school. My schooling expedition started with a lot of unknowns for my parents. Will he do well in school? Will others accept him for who he is? How will teachers react to, or interact with, a student who will need tons of extra guidance in order to understand what is happening around him?

There were so many questions that no one really knew the answer to. I had only one choice each time I started a new school—to put one foot in front of the other and walk through those huge doors. The unknowns were about to become known.

Starting elementary school was the smoothest transition of all my schooling. I went through various changes in middle school and high school. Some of these were easier than others, each having its own positive and negative experiences, just like life itself. I view my schooling experiences much like the personal experiences I've endured in life. Some days are better than others; some days you feel temptation to give up, throw in the towel and say, "I QUIT!" You think to yourself, "I cannot do this anymore. Why can I understand this but have such a hard time grasping the meaning of what I'm reading on a sheet of paper?" Oftentimes, you erase your answer more times than you care to remember, but you finally get the right answer—smiles all around. You treat yourself with some type of reward. After all, you did eventually get it right no matter how many times you used that damn eraser.

It's the same thing with life. Nothing will ever go perfectly. Nothing will be handed to you. God molded us as human beings and wants us to show Him we believe in ourselves, no matter how many times we fall or fail. So, dust yourself off and start over. He believes in you and you should believe in yourself. Having a bad day at work? Can't do the things you wish you could do that others can? The solution itself is quite simple. Instead of dwelling on what you cannot do or the things you wish you could take back, use that as motivation you can apply to your life. Take the motivation you have been given by God to try something new that is out of your comfort zone.

The "eraser" holds all the things that some people cannot do physically, emotionally, or mentally. Use that eraser and sharpen your ability—your "pencil"—to try new things. These can be things that make you nervous or uncomfortable. You see, you may be unable to do 100 things in life, but use God and your own life as motivation to prove to yourself, those around you, and especially Him, that you CAN do 200 other things just as well. Use the eraser, but think with the pencil of life to come up with the things that make God proud.

I've followed this method for 31 plus years. That's 11,315 plus days. Believe in yourself and let your faith in God show. Smile and let your courageous spirit take you to the many places in the life that you've been given—not just to make yourself proud, but also those around you and Him.

THINK | PRAY | MEDITATE

It constantly amazes me that men and women wander the earth marveling at the highest mountains, the deepest ocean, the whitest sands, the most exotic islands, the most intriguing birds of the air and fish of the sea - and all the time never stop to marvel at themselves and realize their infinite potential as human beings.

— Matthew Kelly

CHAPTER FIVE: CP

CENTER ADVENTURE

I can do all this through him who gives me strength.

Philippians 4:13

LEARNING DURING MY EARLY years took place at the wonderful CP Center in Green Bay. This center helped all kinds of differently abled people of varying ages and needs. Some days were easier than others, but the center had a huge impact on me and my family and it continues to hold a special place in my heart.

One of the stories I was frequently told involved my water therapy there. Physical therapy wasn't always the easiest for me, especially as a young boy. In the car on the way to the center, I would recognize where I was going and begin to bawl. My crying continued and caused me to throw up in the pool I was using for therapy. My mother couldn't bear to watch my distress in the center, so Dr. Winston, my NICU doctor, had my therapy moved to my home.

When I got a little older, I returned to the CP Center and accomplished as much as I could, with and without help. Through the aches and pains, but with a strong desire not to quit, I learned to walk! In fact, at its annual CP Telethon, I walked on live television at the age of 4. I don't remember this day, but the proof is on the VHS tape on which the telethon is recorded. I must say for all of the struggles I went through, therapy from the CP Center certainly paid off—not only for me and my family, but for everyone who saw this telethon. I can only imagine all the happiness that was felt that day. When I finished walking, the hosts of the show sang Happy Birthday to me.

My family hosted a bowling fundraiser for the CP Center and collected $617. That was a lot of money in 1986, and our event made it on TV.

As difficult as the therapy and expectations were at such a young age, I will forever be grateful to the CP Center and the people who worked alongside me and gave me a jump start on accomplishing the little things, but most importantly, the big thing—walking!

THINK | PRAY | MEDITATE

If God had a refrigerator, your picture would be on it. If He had a wallet, your photo would be in it. He sends you flowers every spring and a sunrise every morning... Face it, friend. He is crazy about you!

— Max Lucado

CHAPTER SIX: STEPPING STONES

So then, just as you received Christ Jesus as Lord, continue to live your lives in him, rooted and built up in him, strengthened in the faith as you were taught, and overflowing with thankfulness.

Colossians 2:6-7

EVEN BEFORE I STARTED my elementary school journey, my family and I made a few "pit stops." It was a way to use all of the resources available to make moving forward as a kid a bit easier on all of us. Looking back, I'm sure glad we worked as a team to help my schooling go smoothly. It benefited me on all fronts, physically and emotionally, and it gave me the ability to take that first step.

One of my first schools was the Sullivan Elementary School in Green Bay. The staff wanted me to enjoy being a kid but at the same time taught me to see myself as differently ABLED so that I could be as independent as possible.

This was the start of my therapy journey, which continued up to high school. My team focused on both my occupational needs and physical needs. It was a lot of work for a kid, and I didn't always like it, but my family knew I needed this support so we went through it together.

Many of my first stepping stones were positive. My mother tells me that when the bus picked me up to go to school, I got on gleefully without even a question for her. But while I was being adventurous and independent riding to Sullivan School, she was crying. I hope it was a good cry because this was my first real step forward in my education. I learned to be happy and to adapt, even on the difficult days that I endured.

I liked every aspect of this school despite having to wear braces or splints on my left hand and left foot in an effort to straighten them. The splints were downright ugly. Most were made of plastic and had straps to keep them secure. I may not have liked them, but they did wonders and straightened my entire arm and my foot. Unfortunately, I still cannot turn my left wrist, which tends to turn on its own.

I will never forget the people of Sullivan School who put their blood, sweat, and tears into helping little Joey. The effort they put into helping my body stay as stable as possible is something I will always treasure. I think about the people of Sullivan School a lot, and without them, my school journey would have been a lot rougher.

THINK | PRAY | MEDITATE

Don't ask yourself what the world needs, ask yourself what makes you come alive, because what the world needs are men who have come alive.

— John Eldredge

CHAPTER SEVEN:

KENNEDY ELEMENTARY

The Lord is my shepherd, I lack nothing.
He makes me lie down in green pastures,
he leads me beside quiet waters,
he refreshes my soul.
He guides me along the right paths
for his name's sake.
Even though I walk
through the darkest valley, [a]
I will fear no evil,
for you are with me;
your rod and your staff,
they comfort me.

You prepare a table before me
in the presence of my enemies.

You anoint my head with oil;
   my cup overflows.
Surely your goodness and love will follow me
   all the days of my life,
and I will dwell in the house of the Lord
   forever.

Psalm 23

W HEN I FINISHED MY therapy at Sullivan School, I
was ready for Kennedy Elementary and another
school bus. Many of the kids on the bus where strangers to
me. If they saw my parents, these children would ask them
a million questions about the way I looked or walked. My
parents simply answered that I was "different." But two
girls, Lauren and Crystal, went beyond just asking questions. They decided to take me under their wing and make
this journey a bit more comfortable for me.

Together, Lauren and Crystal learned how to strap me
into my bus seat. Some days I walked onto the bus while
other days I used a wheelchair. The girls were dependable,
which was a relief to my family. I was nervous and quite
shy, but once my new friends got me to open up and talk,
I felt included and just like one of the kids. Knowing that
the minute I got on that school bus I would be cared for
by people I could count on made the nervousness go away.
The ride to school wasn't easy in the beginning, but once
we got to know each other, we learned that looks don't
matter when it comes to making friends.

I remember stepping off the bus and walking into the
school the first time. I saw freshly cleaned floors, coat
hangers, and new faces. The teachers met me with a smile

and helped me find my classroom. It's good to remember how calm I was at this new school. I was now a Cobra, the Kennedy School mascot, for life.

The most interesting thing about this school was that some of the students were hard of hearing while others were deaf and still others had no hearing impairment. Did it scare me a bit? You're darn right it did. I wondered, how does a person communicate around here? Here is the thing, though. I was never really 100% hearing abled, but I wasn't completely deaf. At the time, my hearing was measured as 75% in each ear. Unfortunately, in the years ahead I would lose much of that hearing ability.

At Kennedy, I learned a beautiful new language, American Sign Language. It was astonishing! I could now communicate in two ways, using sign language and my words. Every day, we had short sign language lessons and learned more signs and better ways to communicate. What was even better was it didn't matter if the person I was communicating with was hearing, hard of hearing, or deaf. I could carry on a conversation, no problem.

We were also taught how to wear Assisted Listening Devices or ALDs. The student wore a box-like device that was strapped around the body as well as a hearing aid, and the teacher communicated through a microphone that transported sound to it. The ALDs didn't always work, and I didn't always like them, but most of the time I could understand the teacher better, which was wonderful. Some classrooms had sign language interpreters for the deaf and hard-of-hearing students. Having an interpreter helped me; especially when my ALD wouldn't function.

One of my biggest hurtles with hearing and speaking was telling the difference between high and low pitches. Because of this, I received speech therapy. Because only one side of my body was physically abled, I also received physical and occupational therapy. I didn't care for any of these services, but in the long run, they made all the difference in the world.

Going into elementary school, you start out with many strangers before you have friends. There are people you don't know but whom you need to get to know. I made a lot of friends at this school but there was one guy who stood out. His name was Travis and he was my first "real" friend at school.

Travis and I began as complete strangers. But the more we got to know each other, the more comfortable I felt. He made me feel like everything was going to be OK. I didn't need to be scared or afraid of anything. Once we got to know each other on a more personal level, I realized he didn't care how I looked. He made sure I made it to class and always asked if I needed help here or there. We were on Student Council together. Outside of school, we got to know each other's families. We went to each other's homes. Heck, we even liked the same football team at the time, the Dallas Cowboys. Travis was everything I could ever ask for in a friend, and more. The cool part about this friendship? We still keep in touch today. Thank you, Travis, for being my friend.

I was really pleased with this school environment because no matter what your hearing or physical situation was, you were included—from the time the morning bell rang through after-school hours. You didn't need to go ask to be part of something—you simply signed up and you were in. I enjoyed Student Council because I was able to find out all the happenings at school from fundraisers to Popcorn Day.

One of my medical conditions, a seizure disorder, began at Kennedy. That day we were at odd-shaped tables and had pizza slices cut in the shape of rectangles and served in steaming plastic bags that were so hot we had to wait for the pizza to cool before we could eat it. When I sat down I felt my left hand start to shake. I got up and walked to the principal, Mr. Zegers, who was standing in the middle of the lunchroom (converted from the gym) and told him something was wrong with my hand.

He sat me down at a table outside the lunchroom and paged Miss Nelson, one of the paraprofessionals who worked with me. That is the last thing I remember before waking up in the hospital with her standing next to my bed. My mother was also there. I was later told that the seizure seemed to last quite a while, prompting the school to call 911 and my mother. My mother had just returned home from the grocery store. She dropped her bags and sped to the hospital.

Miss Nelson rode with me in the ambulance. I don't remember the details of what she did or how she did it, but I suspect that if it weren't for her heroic actions that day, the situation would have turned out quite differently. I consider her my lifesaver.

When I returned home, I had four bandages down my arm where I had been given injections. I also had lots of thoughts swirling in my head that I needed to sort through.

Despite these kinds of hurdles, my schooling seemed to me to be basically worry free and I had everything going in the right direction. I always put one foot in front of the other. Every morning I got on that bus and entered that school building. Much like life itself, the unknowns will not be known until you take that first step—in only one direction—forward.

THINK | PRAY | MEDITATE

Make Me an Instrument of Your Peace

Lord, make me an instrument of your peace.
Where there is hatred, let me sow love,
Where there is injury, pardon
Where there is doubt, faith,
Where there is despair, hope,
Where there is darkness, light,
Where there is sadness, joy.
O Divine Master, grant that I may not so much
seek to be consoled as to console,
not so much to be understood as to understand,
not so much to be loved, as to love;
for it is in giving that we receive,
it is in pardoning that we are pardoned,
it is in dying that we awake to eternal life.

— St. Francis of Assisi

CHAPTER EIGHT:

SCOLIOSIS SURGERY

So do not fear, for I am with you;
  do not be dismayed, for I am your God.
I will strengthen you and help you;
  I will uphold you with my righteous right hand.

Isaiah 41:10

I'VE HAD SO MANY surgeries that I've lost count. But the surgery to correct scoliosis, the curvature of my spine, stands out as the most challenging of them all because I had to give everything I had to get back to where I was prior to the operation.

The problem was detected when I was 10 years old when my physical therapist noticed that my walking was deteriorating. My family made an appointment with a local doctor, which led to a trip to one of the most prestigious hospitals in the country, Children's Minnesota, the children's hospital in Saint Paul.

Being just a child at the time, I assumed I was going for a routine checkup. To me it was just another day with another doctor. I'm not sure what my family's thoughts were before the appointment, but I can't imagine they expected to hear good news.

My mom, Aunt Debbie, Aunt Doreen, and my Grandma Marge went with me to Minnesota in September. After extensive testing, Dr. Denis showed us an x-ray that revealed my sternum was pushing against my heart. We stayed overnight in Saint Paul so I could be seen the next day by heart specialist Dr. Lyon.

We didn't have much time to process the situation when it was determined that surgery was my best option. On the x-ray, my spine looked like a snake twisting and twirling down my entire back. We discussed waiting a couple years until I was more fully grown, but due to the severity of the situation, the doctors decided surgery could not wait. I was fearful and broke down in tears, but I found comfort in my family.

The Friday before we left for the surgery in Minnesota, my teachers and classmates had a surprise sendoff for me. They gave me a number of presents including handheld electronic games and Dallas Cowboys memorabilia. The Cowboys may have been my favorite football team, but my favorite NFL player was Reggie White, Green Bay Number 92, the Minister of Defense. I was told he had been invited to the party but wasn't able to make it. Instead, he signed a plaque for me.

It was a terrific party filled with joy, excitement, and

tears shared with my family, the principal, and my class-mates. We took a lot of photos (which now fill a scrapbook), and I knew I was going to miss every single person in that classroom.

That night, the phone rang at my house. I was asleep but my sisters woke me up to tell me the call was for me. It was very late, but I managed to answer the phone and heard the voice of Mr. Reggie White himself! I was ecstatic and overjoyed that an actual Packer player, let alone my favorite one, personally called me to wish me well on my surgery. I will never ever forget that party or phone call. They made a young kid feel so special!

My mom and I flew to the Twin Cities for the operation the next morning. My mom's friend Julie came to Saint Paul that afternoon, which helped calm my mom's nerves. We all went to the Mall of America and had dinner at The Rainforest Café where the sights and sounds of the jungle turned the medical trip into a fun adventure.

The following day my Aunt Debbie arrived, and my support team was on the job. Even though I was only 10, I understood the surgery would improve my diagnosis, and so I was optimistic.

We headed to the hospital very early the following morning. With my stuffed bumble bee "Buzzy," I was wheeled into the operating room at 6 a.m. My mom was able to accompany me briefly into the room. It made me smile to see her in a surgical gown, cap, and plastic-covered shoes. But then she left so the surgery could begin.

Staff members gave my mom a beeper so she could receive progress reports. For 10 ½ hours she did the best she could to remain calm. The surgeons intentionally broke my spine and inserted thirteen rods with screws into it. The hardware began at the top of my neck and ended at my tailbone.

Just a few days after my spinal surgery, I was scheduled for an operation on my sternum. The surgery was initially scheduled for three days post-op, but it was determined I wasn't strong enough then. On the fifth day, the surgical team was given the go-ahead and I was again brought into the operating room. My sternum was caving in and pressing against my chest cavity. An entire fist could fit inside my chest. The team of doctors broke my sternum and proceeded to pull it out to line up with the rest of my body. With two major surgeries completed in five days, I could finally begin my recovery.

I remained at Children's for two weeks. Being unable to move and confined to a hospital bed was difficult, but many family members made the trip to Minnesota to visit me, and my friends and teachers from Kennedy Elementary created handmade cards that decorated my room and lifted my spirits.

A steady stream of doctors, nurses, and therapists also visited me. I received respiratory therapy around the clock to strengthen my lungs. I would jokingly complain about being woken up. But I knew I couldn't go home if I wasn't healthy, so my love/hate relationship with respiratory therapy ended with nothing but love.

I had an amazing team, but one resident stood out. His name was Dr. Matt. He was the one who most often woke me in the middle of the night, but he had a fun way of keeping me at ease. Under his hospital coat he wore a long-sleeved shirt decorated with flames, which I thought was awesome. During my recovery at Children's, the Green Bay Packers were playing the Dallas Cowboys. Dr. Matt despised the Cowboys and was confident the Packers would win, while I, a die-hard Cowboys fan, was convinced the Cowboys would be victorious. He wagered that if the Cowboys won the game he would wear a "Cowboys Rule!" sign on his back. The Cowboys did in fact beat the Packers, and Dr. Matt walked around with that sign on his back. It's amazing what a resident will do to make a patient smile, and believe me, I was grinning from ear to ear.

Before I left the hospital, I was fitted for a body brace, which I had to wear for the next two months. The brace had a metal wire that stuck out and went into my sternum. It helped keep my sternum pulled forward. By this point in my life I had worn arm and leg braces, but they were nothing compared to the body brace. I slept in my wheelchair because I couldn't move very much. I used pillows and blankets for support and comfort. At times, laughing hurt. I grew increasingly frustrated on the days I was unable to find a comfortable position to sit or lie. It was a long two months.

The day finally arrived to have the body brace removed. I was excited yet anxious because I had no idea how a body brace with a metal wire stuck into my sternum was going to be removed. My mom and I went to see Dr. Lyons. He took out an instrument similar to a pair of pliers and attached it to the metal piece that was in my sternum. I remember him telling me it was going to hurt. On the count of three he was going to pull the metal piece out. Together we counted to three and I let out the loudest scream I have ever produced. After that scream, I knew I could focus on getting back to my normal self: no metal stuck into my sternum, no more sleepless nights. I had to wear the body brace for another two months or so to keep my back straight. I still have the brace today, and I cringe every time I look at it.

Surgery for scoliosis wasn't easy to go through, but no surgery is. Looking back, I'm grateful my family members followed through and listened to my therapist. I don't know where I would be today if they had not. I am forever proud to have made it through a tough surgery. I appreciate every person involved and cannot thank my family enough for having the problem fixed rather than ignored. And I thank God for watching over me and ensuring my family remained at ease as our faith strengthened.

THINK | PRAY | MEDITATE

The Irish Blessing

May the road rise to meet you,
May the wind be always at your back,
May the sun shine warm upon your face,
The rains fall soft upon your fields and,
Until we meet again,
May God hold you in the palm of His hand.

CHAPTER NINE: PULASKI

MIDDLE SCHOOL

Trust in the Lord with all your heart
and lean not on your own understanding;
in all your ways submit to him,
and he will make your paths straight.

Proverbs 3:5-6

THIS PART OF MY schooling—middle school—is where life became tough, very tough. I went from having a group of individuals that I looked up to and trusted and called my friends to being at a whole new school in a new district in a new city.

In 1998, I moved from Green Bay to Pulaski. I was now back at square one. It was like being handed a new puzzle piece and having to do whatever it took to make that piece fit. I was nervous but I had no choice but to try to embrace this new environment.

There were positives, as there always are, such as the challenge to make new friends, meet new teachers, and be optimistic on a daily basis. I did smile and do the best I could every day. But the challenges seemed to grow as my struggles and difficulties increased.

It appeared to me that I was the first, if not the only, differently abled student in the Pulaski School District. No one seemed to know how to handle or help a student who needed extra care and more explanation. This was particularly true when it came to teachers. Teachers needed to adjust to my needs, such as giving me more time to complete my work, providing me with copies of notes, and turning on closed captioning for movies and videos. But some grew impatient with me, and it made my adjustment more difficult.

Things became so difficult that I began to miss school to avoid bothering teachers who were trying to run their classrooms. I didn't want to be a burden. I would cry at home trying to figure out how I would even make it through the first year, much less all of middle school.

I wanted my teachers to embrace the fact that I had trouble but that I was there to learn. I wanted them to teach me in any and all subjects, no matter how long it took. I wanted them to know I was just like any other student. It was going to take time and effort, both physically and mentally, for both student and teacher, but I deserved the same education as my classmates. Once we found the right approach for both the learner and the teacher, we found common ground. As time went on, I actually became their learning tool, and the teachers seemed to adjust to my needs.

I thought about my group of friends from Kennedy Elementary a lot and how much I missed them. Being surrounded by peers I didn't know was daunting for both me and the other students. I tried to put myself in their place. What do you say to a kid who can't do the things you can do, like hear or follow directions without repetition? How do you even introduce yourself to someone that is physically differently abled? I kept quiet and to myself a lot of the time. I did what I was expected to do in class, one assignment after another.

Little by little, I began to accept my new challenges. I decided to force myself to go up to students and interact, just like any other student would. Day by day, the loneliness wore off and my classmates started to respond to me. The astonishing part was when I realized they all were looking past the fact that I only had the use of one side of my body, that I couldn't hear them the first time, and that it took me longer to complete tasks. Some even offered to help me!

Over time, I became comfortable and felt like one of the group. I was included and it felt awesome! Despite my inability to comprehend a specific lesson the first time, or needing help solving a math problem, I was accepted. It was a relief to be accepted for who I was, even while struggling academically, to no longer be lonely with no one to guide me through middle school life.

After the loneliness that I had felt initially, making friends turned out to be one of the best parts of middle school. They were all cool and very accepting of me for being, well, me. But there was one person in particular, Tyler, who made all the difference.

Tyler was in many of my classes and made sure I made

it from point A to point B. We even worked on some school projects together, which is when we got to know each other on a more personal level. The days that I needed a friend, a helping hand, he would be the first one there.

My favorite video gaming system at the time was Nintendo 64 and I loved playing James Bond Golden Eye. One fond memory I have is beating Tyler even though I only had one hand to control the game! Tyler and I are still friends today. I couldn't be more grateful for the years of friendship and his acceptance. Thanks, T!

As with any other student going from elementary to middle school, I felt the stress. The care-free days of elementary school were over. Between the testing, the homework load, and the countless number of projects, I was taken aback. It hit me full force, but I did the work and walked through the storm, no matter how hard it hailed. I finished tests, completed assignments, and turned in projects with pride and a beaming smile.

Like I've said, I love a good challenge, but this one, middle school, was by far my toughest one. Schooling is supposed to be fun, right? But I was born with challenges that I had to overcome. These challenges changed me as a person. I became more accepting, I taught myself to not give up, and, most of all, that no matter how many rugged tracks there are to cross, I'll cross them all. And I did—while smiling.

THINK | PRAY | MEDITATE

We find God, I think, through others – through the love we learn to offer them, through the love we learn to receive from them – no small achievement, and indeed, a lifelong effort. We find God with difficulty – the obstacle of pride is always there, with its various forms of expression: self-preoccupations, self-importance, smugness, arrogance, pretentiousness, in George Eliot's phrase 'unreflecting egoism" – all of that hinders, squelches the movement of the mind, heart and soul outward, toward others, whom we might come to know, trust, love, were we less locked into the prison of the self. God, then, is the great Other, and comes to each of us, lives for each of us, insofar as we can find Him through our daily lives: how they are lived with our fellow human beings.

— Robert Coles

CHAPTER TEN: PULASKI

HIGH SCHOOL

Have I not commanded you? Be strong and courageous.
Do not be afraid; do not be discouraged, for the Lord
your God will be with you wherever you go.

Joshua 1:9

IT'S OFTEN SAID THE four years of high school are the best years of your life. By high school I had adjusted to my new home in the Pulaski School District. I had a set schedule, a routine, and a great group of people supporting me every day.

Walking into high school on that first day, I knew I was going to be OK and make it through the day. I was able to take my experiences from middle school and grow.

I turned struggles into triumphs, and every day was different.

Some of my classmates knew me from middle school, while others were meeting me for the first time. They all had one thing in common—which was heartwarming to not only see but hear—they didn't care what I looked like. It didn't matter to them that I walked with a slight limp or that my left hand looked different from my right. No one spoke a word about it.

Although I was able to walk, my limbs would give out if I walked from morning through the afternoon, so I used a scooter. The scooter was quite large, and other students could see me coming down the hallway from a distance. It had a basket on the front for my backpack and school supplies, but sometimes I had to make multiple trips to haul everything I needed for a class. Not once did another student offer to help me carry anything—and I loved that! They let me do things on my own. If I needed to make two trips, I did. No excuses. That's the triumph! I didn't ask for help, nor did I need it. I had become much more independent and I was able to do things on my own.

Physical therapy sessions continued into high school including during the summer months. When I was a freshman, my therapists organized a summer school program for differently abled students. It was the best! The therapists found creative ways to help us stretch our muscles. For example, they took the older students to the track to ride go-karts. I sat in the go-kart with my legs stretched out to extend my hamstrings. Turning the corners of the track forced me to look both ways and work on my weaker side, and I needed to use both hands to maneuver the steering wheel.

The days were long for therapists Lynn and Mandy, who worked with the younger children in the morning and teenagers like me in the afternoon. Truthfully, I was far ahead of the other students cognitively, but I never once judged them. They were working just as hard as I was, and we supported each other. It was important for the other kids to have someone with physical challenges from whom they could learn.

One particularly tough day was the day I had a seizure. Students from an area technical college were observing the therapy. My seizure was unexpected, as seizures always are, but I took it in stride. After all, I've dealt with worse. That was a learning experience for all of us.

The therapists took a big interest in the children. One even suggested that I consider having surgery to lengthen my hamstrings because they were so tight. At age 14, I went ahead and had the surgery, which was a success.

During the school year, therapy included performing range-of-motion movements to keep mobility on my left side intact and exercising my legs to keep them strong. I was always challenged. Sometimes the therapist had me working on the shoulder region, other times the focus was solely on my legs. Some exercises were done daily, while others I would perform only once before moving on to the next.

I would walk on a treadmill and later walk backwards up the school stairs to strengthen my glutes. Man, did that burn! I also mopped the wrestling floors, which required me to put my thinking cap on as I needed to figure out how to perform the task despite having only one abled side.

Physical therapy kept my body from deteriorating, but, let's face it, I needed occupational therapy as well. I wore a splint on my left hand to keep it from turning inward. In OT sessions we did activities that forced me to open my hand and grab onto things, such as the handlebar of

Friends and teachers were such a delight,
we will remember each other for life.

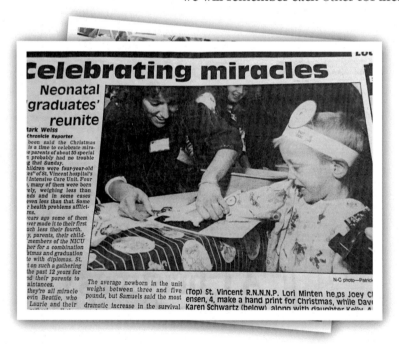

Celebrating my life with others alike
made me feel like my future was bright.

2013 was my first mTT race
only to realize what my body could embrace.

Crossing the finish line one my own two feet,
with the others was such a feat.

Therapy with friends has just begun,
but at the same time, I could have some fun.

Family by my side is always number one,
without them, I wonder what I might have become.

We started as strangers on day one,
but no matter what, our friendship has won.
(Travis & Joe)

Middle school was rough but
we remained friends no matter what.
(Tyler & JC)

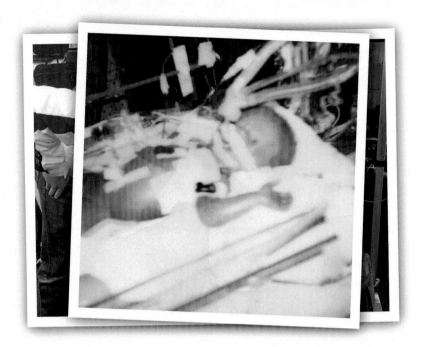

88 days in the NICU,
all ready for the world to experience something new.

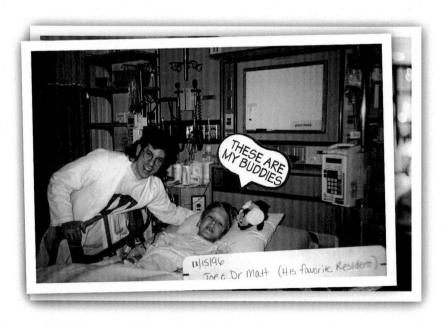

For being stuck in a room for 2 weeks,
seeing Dr. Matt was a great treat.

All hooked up and ready to fight,
we knew the future would be alright.

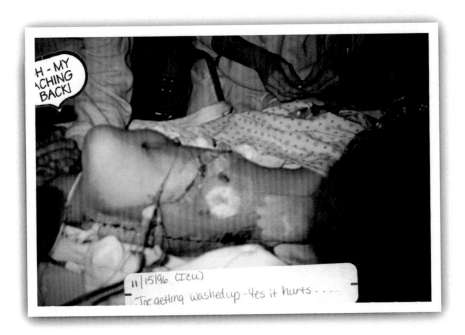

Getting my scars was a hardship of its own,
but keeping them clean kept me in the zone.

Me with mom - looking like a pro -
not knowing where the road will go.

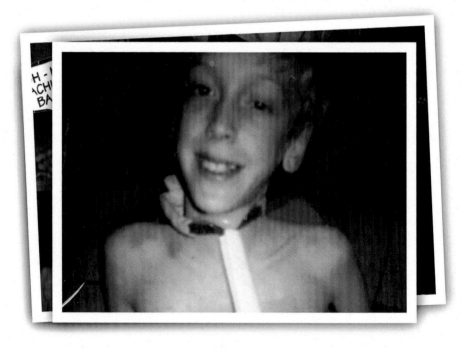

Wearing it was no fun,
but getting better was number one.

4 years old with a smile so bright,
walking on TV was the biggest accomplishment of my young life.

A medical condition that caught everyone off guard,
is now something I live with, with high regards.

Just born, safe and sound,
the storm unknown to everyone around.

I was about to go through the biggest surgery in my life,
my friends were by my side all through the fight.

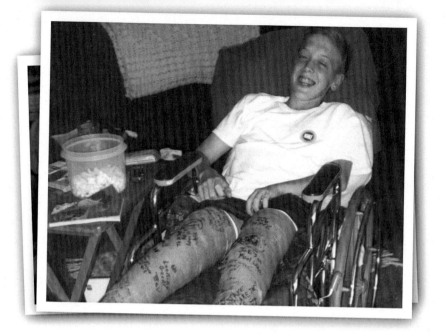

Surgery after surgery they put put me in big casts,
making my tight hamstrings free at last.

Mr Zegers, a man with a big heart,
helped me get rid of all my doubts.
(This doesn't rhyme…but this is my book and I can do what I want!)

an exercise bike.

Occupational therapy allowed me to improve not just physically but mentally. Through the creative use of medicine balls and chairs, the therapists and I worked both sides of my body. Man, what a workout that was for my left side! Despite the hard work, I'm thankful for the movement that allowed me to keep my left side as functional as possible.

To many high school students, going home at the end of the day was the best part of the day. But sometimes I didn't want to go home. Being able to show my peers and teachers my capabilities and share my triumphs, no matter how small they may have been, led to my best four years. I was brave when I was scared, strong when I wanted to be weak, and, most importantly, humble as I accepted obstacles and turned them into victories.

I'd like to thank the therapists who worked with me throughout my school years. In addition to Lynn and Mandy, there were Shawn and Amy and many staff I unfortunately can't remember the names of. Without your guidance and support, I don't think I would have realized just how important therapy is. You guys stuck with me on both my good days and bad, always making me a better person. Because of you, I can proudly say that therapy was life-changing for me. It made me learn more about just what my body could do. From the bottom of my heart, thank you! P.S. I still do home exercises. You'd be mighty proud of me!

THINK | PRAY | MEDITATE

Promise yourself to be so strong that nothing can disturb your peace of mind. Look at the sunny side of everything and make your optimism come true. Think only the best, to work only for the best, and to expect only the best. Forget the mistakes of the past and press on to the greater achievements of the future. Give so much time to the improvement of yourself that you have no time to criticize others. Live in faith that the whole world is on your side so long as you are true to the best that is in you.

— Christian D. Larson

CHAPTER ELEVEN: I WILL

GET THROUGH THIS

Therefore, since we are surrounded by such a great cloud of witnesses, let us throw off everything that hinders and the sin that so easily entangles. And let us run with perseverance the race marked out for us, fixing our eyes on Jesus, the pioneer and perfecter of faith. For the joy set before him he endured the cross, scorning its shame, and sat down at the right hand of the throne of God.

Hebrews 12:1-2

WE MAY THINK OUR God-given life plan will go smoothly, but we often face battles that will turn our smiles into frowns, the light into darkness, and courage into weakness. Life is not, and will never be, a consistent straight line on a smoothly paved road. Each time you're knocked off onto a curving dirt path, you will find that He has a way of showing you that the unexpected only strengthens you and lifts your spirits.

As I have grown I've learned that my heart and mind are connected to my faith. I've learned that no matter the circumstances, I can face my fears with confidence. My faith will forever remain bigger than my fears. Fear is inevitable, but the power of faith in both yourself and in Him will give you all the strength you need to get through.

Growing up I learned to not obsess over the question of can I or can't I. I didn't allow myself to just wonder if I could—I had faith on my side. I found alternative solutions to completing a task.

Opening a bag of chips, buttoning a shirt, or twisting open a bottle of soda are things most people do without thinking twice. I sometimes had to think three or four times about it, but I always found a way. Telling myself I could gave me the strength and determination to never give up. Every time I succeeded, I felt it was a sign from Him reminding me I could accomplish anything.

Everything became a learning process for me. I initially allowed others to do things for me, but as I grew older my desire for independence increased. That's when I turned my mind and body into a learning machine.

Opening a bag of potato chips is an easy task for anyone with two fully functioning hands, but I had to attack it differently. Using my one functioning hand, I took a pair of scissors and sliced the bag wide open. But I was determined to open the bag just as anyone else would, by pulling the precut tab. I placed the bag on my lap and pulled the tab, but that just resulted in popping the bag and crushing everything inside. After numerous attempts and changing my plan, I finally found a method that worked. Grasping the tab with my teeth and pulling the other side with my hand kept the bag from popping! My determination for not using scissors paid off, and I was one happy potato chip-eating boy.

Bathing brought a lot of frustration. I could never get into the shower without holding onto something once my abled leg made it over the side of the tub. I did some research and found exactly what I was looking for in order to adapt to my abilities. My family went ahead and re-modeled the bathroom. A floor-level shower with slip-free tiles was installed, as well as grab bars for stability. With the new seat in the corner of the shower, I can sit down as necessary, and the detachable shower head allows me to rinse myself without having to turn around. Remodeling the bathroom was quite the process, but it paid off. I cannot put a price on how it feels to shower independently and feeling safe while doing so.

Getting dressed is a particularly demanding task when you only have one side of your body to work with. I despised clothing with buttons. A collared button-up shirt was far from my favorite. Knowing I would need to be able to button a shirt at some point in my life, I accepted 6-the challenge. At first I tried using just my fingers in various ways, but I always ended up with a finger slipping from one side when I had to push the other side of the button through the buttonhole. Through trial and error—and my chin—I eventually succeeded. With the shirt on and my chin holding the middle of the shirt down, I could push every one of those buttons through the holes. It may take me a little longer than most to button a shirt, but I can now do it independently, whew!

THINK | PRAY | MEDITATE

There are only two kinds of people: those who say to God, "Thy will be done," and those to whom God says, "All right, then, have it your way."

— C.S. Lewis

CHAPTER TWELVE: MY WILL TO LIVE

For God so loved the world that he gave his one and only Son, that whoever believes in him shall not perish but have eternal life.

John 3:16

MY FAMILY MEMBERS KNEW at birth I would face many hurtles throughout my life, but their support and encouragement have remained constant. They made the best of the situation from the day I was born and continue to do so today.

It began with trusting the medical professionals in the hospital's NICU. When it was time to leave the hospital, no one knew if I would continue to thrive, but my parents soon realized I was a fighter and that somehow, I was going to make it through every hour of every day.

As an infant, I had an apnea monitor wrapped around my chest at night. The machine beeped repetitively if my breathing stopped, and someone would have to check on me. My family members also worked together to ensure I was receiving enough nutrition because my tiny body needed every ounce it could possibly get.

It's clear to me that my family has given me the will to live and, just like when I was small, my loved ones continue to check up on me and nurture me with their care.

Each has had his or her own way of showing me respect and support. Maybe it's a hug, a high five, a text message, a phone call, or a ride to and from rehab—in all ways large and small they have shown me that they know what I'm going through and that I'm not going through it alone.

The obstacles often set me back a bit. The surgeries, therapy, and braces were all "bumps" that I needed to overcome as a child to allow me to become the adult I am today. As a kid, I never thought about it and always wore a smile, but as I grew older I came to understand how these bumps prepared me for life.

For example, consider my hearing loss. I was lucky enough to be placed at Kennedy Elementary where I learned American Sign Language and became friends with hard-of-hearing classmates. My hearing was never perfect. During elementary school, my hearing percentages were usually around 75 percent. But by the time I was 26 years old, I had lost the majority of my hearing in both ears. Upon testing, it was concluded that my hearing was at 16 percent in my left ear and just 12 percent in my right ear. A dramatic change, but my will to never give up remains intact.

Another "bump" I am now thankful for was my need for therapy at a young age. I've undergone at least eight surgeries, and the majority of these required some sort of physical rehabilitation. Because I had physical and occupational therapy when I was just a little boy, I was familiar with rehab and knew my post-surgery efforts would be worth it. I never gave up my will to succeed.

I know the journey I travel will never be easy, but with the support of my family, both those on earth with me and those now with God, I know it will be OK. The pain is eased and the process is smoother. Their love has gotten me through so far and I will persevere.

THINK | PRAY | MEDITATE

Glory Be

Glory be to the Father,
and to the Son,
and to the Holy Spirit,
as it was in the beginning,
is now, and ever shall be,
world without end. Amen.

CHAPTER THIRTEEN: MY FAITH

IN EVERY DAY OF MY LIFE

Come to me, all you who are weary and burdened, and I will give you rest.

Matthew 11:28

G OD GAVE ME THE gift of life and I will get through every day I am given. I have chosen to live my life to its fullest potential. If it weren't for the bad days, I would never know what a good day was!

My faith has shown me that I can step out of my comfort zone. As awkward as it may appear to others, I use my differently abled left arm to the best of its abilities. Lifting, pushing, or even just as support, I wasn't given a left arm for decoration. I've learned it's better to use it than to pretend it's not there.

Having differently abled legs is something I have accepted, and I'm proud to say as an adult I've learned how to adapt. One leg is longer than the other, so with the help of a shoe lift, I'm able to stand up straight without bending my knees. I will always have a slight limp, but I am able to walk. I recently discovered that Nike manufactures LeBron James tennis shoes, which are made for individuals who are differently abled. FlyEase shoes have a zipper across the back near the heel, making it easy to slip them on and off. Not only am I walking in style, I'm walking in shoes made just for me!

I don't take it for granted that I can get dressed, walk from points A to B, brush my teeth, and comb my hair. It may take me a little bit longer than the average person, but because I am here, when the medical prognosis said I shouldn't be, I smile when each task is complete. God is always watching me, I know it for a fact, and I try to make Him proud.

During the good days, I tend to rely less often on people, medicines, and even my breathing products. I can often walk farther without the pit stops, as I call them. I truly believe on my good days that I'm looking up and He is looking down and we are both smiling.

On bad days, my body has to work harder. My breathing may turn into wheezing, which requires me to take more breaks, and I walk less. I dislike these days because my body tends to run out of gas and need to recharge. But I try to remain upbeat, knowing I'll bounce back, and I remember that everyone has bad days, not just the differently abled.

I've always been surrounded by people who express how proud or happy they are with my accomplishments. That gives me the courage to speak about being differently abled and share my journey with people I don't know, and it has also given me the strength to try new things.

I always put my faith in front of me and have learned it's better to accept and pursue a challenge than to sit back in defeat. Waking up and knowing I have one more day added to the timeline of my life inspires me to continue. Taking advantage of life by truly living it is what it's all about. Hearing kind words encourages me to speak kind words. My faith in God has shown me that those in my inner circle were placed there for a reason.

It has also given me the extra strength I need to know that it's OK to have this differently abled life. I feel that God has been with me from the very beginning and still is. His faith in me and my achievements makes my heart grow bigger, my smile grow wider, and my faith grow stronger 24 hours a day, 7 days a week, 365 days a year.

THINK | PRAY | MEDITATE

Will you leave yourself behind if I but call your name?
Will you care for cruel and kind and never be the same?
Will you risk the hostile stare should your life attract or scare?
Will you let me answer prayer in you and you in me?

...

Will you love the "you" you hide if I but call your name?
Will you quell the fear inside and never be the same?
Will you use the faith you've found to reshape the world around, through my sight and touch and sound in you and you in me?

— 'The Summons' by John Bell

CHAPTER FOURTEEN:

MYTEAM TRIUMPH

Do not conform to the pattern of this world, but be transformed by the renewing of your mind. Then you will be able to test and approve what God's will is— his good, pleasing and perfect will.

Romans 12:2

MY FAVORITE SINGER HAS long been Toby Keith. A few years ago, I was lucky enough to attend one of his concerts in Green Bay with my aunt and her friend Sue. Meeting Sue turned out to be one of the best things that ever happened to me because she connected me with a non-profit organization called myTEAM TRIUMPH. I felt the presence of God telling me this was one of my purposes. It was like He took me by the hand and presented me with a reason—a reason for life, while asking me to show Him I could do it.

MyTEAM TRIUMPH was founded by Christian Jensen, his wife Tiffany, and their friend, Mary Cox. Their mission is to enrich the lives of people with diverse abilities by fostering lasting, authentic relationships through the teamwork of endurance athletics. The organization participates in half marathons, full marathons, triathlons, and even Ironman events in Wisconsin and other states. Differently abled individuals, like me, are selected as captains and paired with a team of runners, called Angels, to participate in endurance events.

I was reluctant at first, but decided to at least give it a try. I went to a training run to see what was involved. The differently abled athletes sat in specialized chairs resembling three-wheeled bikes. I sat in one of those chairs for a run or two and sensed a great gasp of energy shooting through my body. I swear it tugged at my heart and actually made it grow. I decided to officially join myTEAM TRIUMPH the next day.

My first official event was the 2013 Bellin Run in Green Bay. To make myself feel more comfortable, I looked for extra Angels to run with me. I asked Sue because she was the one who gave me the push I needed to try something new. I also asked one of my sign language interpreters, Lisa from Kennedy Elementary, and one of her friends who was a runner, Jericho. I completed my first 10K with these extraordinary people. Walking away from that event not only made me happy, but delighted my family as well. I went on to participate in several more races including the Cellcom and Door County half marathons, the Pack 5K, the Bellin Run, and the Brewers Mini-Marathon.

In all honesty, after the Bellin Run I didn't think I would

do much more with this organization despite how much I enjoyed that first event. But, again, the bravery and courage He gave me overpowered the urge to say no. God said try once more, and I continued to try. I was proud of myself, but I was particularly touched that the people who pushed me during these races were also proud.

I continue to be involved in myTEAM TRIUMPH and treasure the friendships, the goals achieved, and the smiles. We call our team The Originals and try to race at least once a year. I've also participated with some of our sponsor teams, which is just as fun.

In 2014, Christian, one of the organization's founders, asked me to be Captain Ambassador, a wonderful honor. I now travel with Christian around Wisconsin and share my life story. Sharing personal details with a group of strangers can be tough, but it's a powerful way for others to realize we are all equal.

I've met many inspiring individuals in this group. Each has his or her own spark. We've grown close and all have nicknames for one another. Because of those I've met through myTEAM TRIUMPH, my life has forever changed. I thank God every day for this great group of people. I'm glad I attended that first training run instead of wondering what could have been. We're all there to help one another learn and grow as people.

To find out more about myTEAM TRIUMPH and what you can do to help yourself or those around you, go to http://myteamtriumph-wi.org. You'll be glad you did.

THE RACE
By Dr. D.H. (Dee) Groberg
Used with Permission

I

"Quit! Give Up! You're beaten!"
They shout at me and plead.
"There's just too much against you now.
This time you can't succeed."

And as I start to hang my head
In front of failure's face,
My downward fall is broken by
The memory of a race.

And hope refills my weakened will
As I recall that scene;
For just the thought of that short race
Rejuvenates my being.

II

A children's race--young boys, young men--
How I remember well.
Excitement, sure! But also fear;
It wasn't hard to tell.

They all lined up so full of hope
Each thought to win that race.
Or tie for first, or if not that,
At least take second place.

And fathers watched from off the side
Each cheering for his son.
And each boy hoped to show his dad
That he would be the one.

The whistle blew and off they went
Young hearts and hopes afire.
To win and be the hero there
Was each young boy's desire.

And one boy in particular
Whose dad was in the crowd
Was running near the lead and thought:
"My did will be so proud!"

But as they speeded down the field
Across a shallow dip,
The little boy who thought to win
Lost his step and slipped.

Trying hard to catch himself
His hands flew out to brace,
And mid the laughter of the crowd
He fell flat on his face.

So down he fell and with him hope
—He couldn't win it now—
Embarrassed, sad, he only wished

To disappear somehow.

But as he fell his dad stood up
And showed his anxious face,
Which to the boy so clearly said,
"Get up and win the race."

He quickly rose, no damage done,
—Behind a bit, that's all—
And ran with all his mind and might
To make up for his fall.

So anxious to restore himself
—To catch up and to win—
His mind went faster than his legs:
He slipped and fell again!

He wished then he had quit before
With only one disgrace.
"I'm hopeless as a runner now;
I shouldn't try to race."

But in the laughing crowd he searched
And found his father's face;
That steady look which said again:
"Get up and win the race!"

So up he jumped to try again
—Ten yards behind the last—
"If I'm to gain those yards," he thought,
"I've got to move real fast."

Exerting everything he had

He regained eight or ten,
But trying so hard to catch the lead
He slipped and fell again!

Defeat! He lied there silently
—A tear dropped from his eye—
"There's no sense running anymore;
Three strikes: I'm out! Why try!"

The will to rise had disappeared;
All hope had fled away;
So far behind, so error prone;
A loser all the way.

"I've lost, so what's the use," he thought
"I'll live with my disgrace."
But then he thought about his dad
Who soon he'd have to face.

"Get up," an echo sounded low.
"Get up and take your place;
You were not meant for failure here.
Get up and win the race."

"With borrowed will get up," it said,
"You haven't lost at all.
For winning is no more than this:
To rise each time you fall."

So up he rose to run once more,
And with a new commit
He resolved that win or lose
At least he wouldn't quit.

So far behind the others now,
—The most he'd ever been—
Still he gave it all he had
And ran as though to win.

Three times he'd fallen, stumbling;
Three times he rose again;
Too far behind to hope to win
He still ran to the end.

They cheered the winning runner
As he crossed the line first place.
Head high, and proud, and happy;
No falling, no disgrace.

But when the fallen youngster
Crossed the line last place,
The crowd gave him the greater cheer,
For finishing the race.

And even though he came in last
With head bowed low, unproud,
You would have thought he'd won the race
To listen to the crowd.

And to his dad he sadly said,
"I didn't do too well."
"To me, you won," his father said.
"You rose each time you fell."

III

And now when things seem dark and hard
And difficult to face,
The memory of that little boy
Helps me in my race.

For all of life is like that race,
With ups and downs and all.
And all you have to do to win,
Is rise each time you fall.

"Quit! Give up! You're beaten!"
They still shout in my face.
But another voice within me says:
"GET UP AND WIN THE RACE!"

CHAPTER FIFTEEN: RESPECT

CAN BE A POWERFUL TOOL

For the word of God is alive and active. Sharper than any double-edged sword, it penetrates even to dividing soul and spirit, joints and marrow; it judges the thoughts and attitudes of the heart.

Hebrews 4:12

WE LEARN NEW THINGS each day of our lives. No matter what our age, there will always be something that will impact us in some new way, shape, or form. It happens when we least expect it.

As someone who is differently abled, I'm aware when people respond negatively to how I look. Staring, laughing, or pointing is demeaning. I'm not doing anything wrong. I am who I am. Happiness isn't gained by enjoying the challenges of others.

Able-bodied people often immediately focus on a person's exterior. But we were all created by the same God, and we will be welcomed back into His arms one day. We all have unique characteristics—we look different or complete tasks in different ways. But what we do have in common is a brain, and we must use it to not only be the best to our God-given ability but also to act in the kindest way possible.

Respect for yourself and for those around you is a powerful tool. I have a tremendous amount of respect for myself, and each day that respect grows a bit more. But there are always going to be individuals who need to be reminded that how they treat me, and others like me, can bring us closer to just giving up. Place yourself in another person's shoes—perspective leads to respect.

How you interact with those of us who are physically differently abled has a giant impact on us. We may be limping or using a wheelchair, but interacting with others has a lot of meaning to us. We know it may be difficult at first, but try. Wouldn't you rather try and make a difference, even in the smallest of ways, than not try and never know? The most rewarding part of interacting with others is that you made it happen. Because of you, we tried.

Always know that it's OK to be unsure at first. Everybody is and will be, no matter who we are. But the more we learn about and from each other, the better. We may start out slow and steady, but before you know it, a friendship is created. Trust me, it does happen. It happened to me with several people who impacted my life in ways they will never even know. But the more we learn about one another, and the more stories we share, the better we become.

We all like to be treated as equals: equal respect, equal love, equal passion, equal opportunities. God created us, He gave us life, and He treats us with respect.

THINK | PRAY | MEDITATE

Hail Mary

Hail Mary, full of grace. The Lord is with thee.
Blessed art thou amongst women,
and blessed is the fruit of thy womb, Jesus.
Holy Mary, Mother of God,
pray for us sinners,
now and at the hour of our death. Amen.

CHAPTER SIXTEEN: CEREBRAL PALSY MAKES ME A FIGHTER

For it is by grace you have been saved, through faith—and this is not from yourselves, it is the gift of God—

Ephesians 2:8

MANY PEOPLE THINK THAT having any medical condition, visible or not, makes them weaker. Individuals think less of themselves. They often wonder, why? Why do I have to have this or deal with all of the stuff that comes with it? They often become alone, isolated, and left out of things.

No matter what the medical condition is, we need to remember one thing: Even though we cannot change our circumstance, we need to embrace it and find out how this can empower us instead of weaken us. Medically, it may not be a choice, but with God and supportive people in our circle, everything will be OK.

I've found this to be true to the very end of every day, whether it be a good day or a bad one. In my case, one medical condition I have no choice but to embrace is Cerebral Palsy. I have what is called Hemiplegia CP, which affects one arm and one leg on the same side of my body. My left side is differently abled, while my right is abled. It's something that is just there. I can't wake up one day and ask God for a new left side. I cannot ask for a do over. What I can do is use it to the best of my given ability. It's there so I might as well use it, right? I refuse to let it just sit there and stare at it every day. I want to make it as able as humanly possible.

So, how do I do that? This is where I put my brain to work. It's something I think about every day, every hour. My brain is always working, sometimes too much, I'm learning. That is the inspiring part.

For example, when I need to lift and move an object from one point to another, I assess the situation. When I was in school, I needed to figure out how to carry my backpack. Carrying it on both shoulders would have been torture for my back muscles and spine. I concluded that I could knot the two shoulder straps together and carry the entire thing on my right side, no matter the weight. Score: Backpack, 0; Joey,1. I was winning, thanks to my creative thinking.

Now, envision a box, taped up and not opened, and weighing 3 to 5 pounds. May not seem like a lot, but when you only have one side to work with, it is. I've been in this situation many times. You know what my brain said? Use your other body parts—your legs! I pushed with my feet forward to straighten the box, leaning down and using my right hand

and palm as support to move the box forward, and went on repeat. This went on until I got the box to its destination. I felt all muscles working! Mission accomplished!

Cerebral Palsy doesn't take away my God-given ability to achieve things. We need to use the things we have in life instead of dwelling on the things we don't have or weren't given. CP makes me a warrior as my body and my inner soul work together to adjust 24 hours a day.

We, as men and women, need to be thankful for any medical conditions that make us fight every day. It is God's way of telling us, "I gave you a battle, now show me you can beat this. I know you can." For me, Cerebral Palsy is just one battle I am fighting and, so far, I'm beating it. I'm taking the reins of my life. You should do the same. Why? Because the outcomes are amazing.

THINK | PRAY | MEDITATE

Saint Michael Prayer

Saint Michael, the Archangel, defend us in battle.
Be our protection against the wickedness and snares of the
devil.
May God rebuke him, we humbly pray;
and do thou, O Prince of the heavenly host,
by the power of God
cast into hell Satan and all the evil spirits
who prowl throughout the world seeking the ruin of souls.
Amen.

CHAPTER SEVENTEEN:

LEADING BY EXAMPLE

*For I am with you, and no one is going to attack and
harm you, because I have many people in this city.*

Acts 18:10

ONE THING I CAN do, and will always do, is lead. I
love the fact that I can use being differently abled to
make positive change as a leader. True, I can't drive, but
does that mean life is over? Absolutely not! I can still get
where I need to go and am not stuck in one place all the
time. I have great surroundings with some pretty amazing
people.

I cannot hear. I'll admit that slowly losing my hearing
was a bitter pill to swallow and accept for a while. But

I refused to sink, give up, and quit. I knew there were brighter days ahead.

I've learned how to use such technology as hearing aids, closed captioning TV, and Bluetooth-assisted equipment in addition to reading lips. Where there is a will, there is a way.

Being born prematurely can be difficult for many. But I now speak to kids of all ages about how to treat others, especially those of us who are differently abled. The key is to help others feel included instead of excluded. It really has been a learning experience, but it is for the good. I take medicine and visit doctors here and there, but who cares, I am here!

Make the most of your God-given situation. Make those around you proud. Make God know that even though it may be difficult at times, you are a happy person and making the best of what He gave you.

You may not see it at first, but those around you are watching. They see how you act, but more importantly, how you react, to each and every situation you are in. One thing to remember is this: you are loved. Take that and use it to the best of your ability. I have. My question for you is, will you?

THINK | PRAY | MEDITATE

But Jesus accepts what we give, blesses it, breaks it open, and magnifies it. Often in ways that we don't see or cannot see. Or will not be able to see in this lifetime. Who knows what a kind word does? Who knows what a single act of charity will do? Sometimes the smallest word or gesture can change a life.

— James Martin

CHAPTER EIGHTEEN:

WHO I AM TODAY

One of the teachers of the law came and heard them debating. Noticing that Jesus had given them a good answer, he asked him, "Of all the commandments, which is the most important?"

"The most important one," answered Jesus, "is this: 'Hear, O Israel: The Lord our God, the Lord is one. Love the Lord your God with all your heart and with all your soul and with all your mind and with all your strength.' The second is this: 'Love your neighbor as yourself.' There is no commandment greater than these."

Mark 12: 28-31

TODAY, I STAND BEFORE myself, those around me, and especially, God, as a 31-year-old man who continues to fight a very difficult battle. I was not supposed to make it past my birthdate and, by all medical expectations, shouldn't be doing a lot of the things I am. Yet, I smile with a grateful heart.

I have learned that being differently abled has made me who I am. I have overcome so many obstacles that I've lost count. It's truly a blessing from Him to be standing here today, alive, with a beating heart and a life full of God's great riches. He was ready for me on March 4, 1986, and He still stands with me.

One of the most challenging courses He has put me through has been surgery. I have endured surgery from the most basic ankle-straightening procedure, to eye surgery, to a challenging scoliosis operation. Some were huge successes, while some didn't work in the long run as well as medical professionals had hoped. While each surgery had its ups and downs, I always came out stronger. My spirit was awoken every time I woke from anesthesia, and God strengthened that spirit to help me become a better person. I know He has been with me every step of the way, making sure I never gave up on myself.

I may not put in typical 40-hour work weeks, but I've worked. I was a cashier at a hardware store, I've done engraving for my mother's trophy business, and taken on data entry for local bowling alleys. I continue to serve as Captain Ambassador for myTEAM TRIUMPH.

As I've grown older, I've felt the need to share my story. Through my organization, Handicapped from the Heart, I speak in schools throughout Wisconsin about my journey. I believe one of my purposes is to share the challenges I have faced by bringing light to them. God's purpose for me is to take this story and run with it. Share it. Let it lift and encourage others.

God may not have given me a fully functioning left side, but He gave me a heartbeat. He has molded me from birth into who I am today. I am far from perfect, but I am here. Through His hands, His spirit, and His guidance, miracles happen. Trust in God and everything will happen for the good. I know I do. Thank you, God, for this blessing of life. I will never be able to thank you enough.

Gracious and loving God,

As I begin this new day, help me to appreciate the importance of living in the here-and-now, not hoping for tomorrow or worrying about yesterday.

Expect me to be a son who honors his parents, a brother who sets the example, a husband who adores his wife, a father who cherishes his children, and a man who seeks to do your will.

Support my efforts to be an instrument of your peace, a friend to the lonely, a host to the poor, and a voice for those whose words have fallen on deaf ears.

Challenge me to live a life whereby others might be able to recognize your goodness in me, just as I am able to find you in them.

Grant me the courage to proclaim proudly and boldly my faith to any person, in any place, at any time.

Keep me forever in your living care and continue to be my guiding light on my journey back to you.

I pray this in your name. Amen.
Mother Mary, pray for me.

— Personal Prayer and Mission of Travis J. Vanden Heuvel

Throughout One More Day, Joe tells us about his family and friends, his teachers and care givers, and the impact they had on his life. "How great would it be," we thought, "if we gave these people an opportunity to tell Joe how much he's impacted their lives?"

My years knowing Joe may not be high in number, but the impact that he has had on my life is quite astonishing. I met Joe just a few short years ago, and we have since participated in a number of events together, from fund raisers, raises, celebrations, etc. From the very beginning, he has always been an upbeat guy, with a heart of gold. I was always shocked at how someone who has been through so much, and has endured more struggle than most could imagine, could be so cheerful and positive. After initially hearing his story, and listening to the heartfelt emotion come through his voice, it was clear that my life would not be the same. A heart string was pulled that had never been touched before. Joe never lets his past, or his struggles, stop him from sharing not only his story, but the stories of many others. He is truly an inspiration, and the work that he does with MyTeam Triumph – WI Chapter is a blessing. It's all about illustrating the abilities, and not letting a disability define you. Everyone has their struggles and hardships in life, but its embracing the positive energy, and the strength of a community that truly makes a difference. Joe has perfected the art form of harnessing that energy, and dispersing it among a group of like-minded individuals looking to spread awareness, and redefine the meaning of achieve. Each time I see Joe, I see his strength and perseverance, and hope to someday get to that level. It is an honor to have met Joe, and I look forward to the many years of friendship ahead. God Bless, and thank you for all you have done. I look forward to witnessing your continued success, and am confident that you will impact many others the way you impacted me.

Sincerely,
Mitch Babe
mTT Angel

***

I met Joe in 2015. That year, My Team Triumph was the recipient of Schreiber's community fundraising.

I had seen My Team Triumph at my, very first, Bellin race in 2010, and knew instantly I had to be a part of what this selfless group of people were doing for the differently abled person in the chair.

It came full circle in 2015 when Christian Jensen and Joe came to share information, with Schreiber, about MTT. At that point, I knew in my heart, this was an organization I could be passionate about, and that I had to run with this incredibly sweet guy Joe, aka Joey Pancakes, Joey Roadshow!

Thus far Joe and I ran the Brewer 1/2 marathon, Door County 1/2 marathon, and this year will run the Bellin and his first marathon. The Fox Cities Marathon.

Joe is not supposed to be here but through his determination and God's grace he is. Joe is thankful for everyday and inspires everyone he meets to live life to the fullest, live in the moment, and be grateful for what you have, even if it's less than ideal.

Thank you Joe for your tremendous inspiration and congratulations on writing your life story that will be sure to touch so many hearts for years to come.

Love Always,

Julie Michiels
mTT Angel

***

Joe,

You've impacted my life from day one, March 4,1986 as neither of us was supposed to live to see March 5,1986. You fought your way into this world, way too early, and you continue that strong fight today with such a strong positive attitude-you are my super hero! You took years off my life that year but the way you continued to fight and win and accomplish things we were told you'd never accomplish. Every obstacle you've encountered in life you've conquered and became a stronger person each time. You've taught me and your whole family to appreciate everything we have and how to deal with things we face in life with a positive attitude- the positive attitude you have had since you entered into this world. I've never, not once heard you complain about anything and you've had every reason to complain with all the obstacles you've encountered. The only time you complained is when you thought you could've done something better! You but that huge light up my life smile on your face and you continue to move forward in life with your strong positive attitude I've ever seen! You, my hero, touch so many people it just amazes me. I get compliments on you all the time-that smile gets to everyone. I lost a lot of faith in 1986 watching you suffer time and time again. But you just kept pushing and overcoming every obstacle you encountered. Gramma Marge helped me regain some faith when she told me " God only gives a special child to someone who can handle them". Well you've given me a lot to handle but today I feel like I am the most blessed mom to have you as my son, my hero. I'm so very proud of you Joey and I will always be at your side as we continue this wonderful special journey in life together. You are the strongest most amazing person I know and I'm so proud to have my Hero at my side everyday. Together we can conquer anything Joey and thank you for that!

You'll always be my hero in life!

Love,
Mom

Dee McKeefry
Joe's mom

***

Joe,

When I think back to the beginning when you were born, it almost seems unreal. What your mom had to go through to get someone to listen, and then the fight you had from the moment you were born; that in itself is an amazing story. As a pediatric nurse I, more than most, understood the challenges you faced, the almost unbelievable way you overcame each surgery, illness, and setback. Always with a smile. Always with no complaints. Always with compassion for others and gratitude for the little we could do for you. When they asked me to write this letter about how you influenced me and my family I thought "where do I start". You taught my children that all people are just people. "Differently abled" is just that. Largely because of you they see people just as people, not as disabled people, just people. Yet since you spent so much time with us when they were young they are kinder when people need help.

If someone needs a hand up, assistance hearing/seeing,

they help without thinking, without realizing it, while still respecting an individuals need to try it on their own. You taught them that. For me Joe, you fill my heart. You make me a better nurse. I can help the families I work with SO much better because I have you. I can help their parents more because of your mom. I have a greater understanding of their needs. I couldn't do my job if it weren't for you. You also give me strength. When I'm tired, hurting, struggling I often think of you. Your strength and positive attitude make me take a deep breath and realize I am blessed. God gave you to us for a reason. The joy, strength and inspiration you give each of us is a true gift from him, and I thank him for that. But most of all Joe, you make me smile. Every time I see you I leave with a smile on my face. You make me laugh. You give me joy. How can I ever thank you for that? Thank you Joe for being you. You make the world a better place and those of us that had the opportunity to have you in our life will be grateful forever.

Love you, Joe!

Debbie Stein
Joe's aunt

***

I've always know how fortunate I was to have Joey in my life but I never knew how true that was until I had kids. He has taught us more about unconditional love than I have ever thought possible. He is strong, caring, selfless and thoughtful in ways I could never teach my kids. He makes me strive to be a better person and mom because of that. He has made my children so accepting and empathetic to other differently abled people. My kids look at him as if he is super human(well he probably is!) In fact some days my kids prefer hugs and high fives from him over us(although I don't like giving him high fives because he likes to remind me his right arm is stronger than both of mine put together!!) I am blessed everyday knowing that my kids and I have him in our lives and I can't really express in words what he means to us or how he's shaped us into the people we are. I can only say thank you which will never be enough. We love you more each day, even if you like to remind me weekly of how many grey hairs I have! We are so lucky as a family to call him ours. We love you more than you will ever know ❤

Jenny Thomson
Joe's Sister

***

Harry,

I've had the privilege of living with the strongest person I have ever met for 20 plus years. There wasn't a day that went by where Joe wasn't smiling from ear to ear, or putting smiles on everyone's face. The kid has the most positive outlook on life I've ever seen. He takes the curveballs that life throws at him, and hits them out of the park. Not only is he the happiest person I know, but he is also the most inspirational. Joe doesn't dream, he does. So now he goes around and inspires little kids from school to school showing them that it doesn't matter your shape or size, you can accomplish anything. He shows them that they can overcome any difficult task that they encounter.

Joe shows them the value of love, kindness, and laughter.

He is a great example of what the word courage is and stands for. If you tried telling him that he couldn't climb Mount Everest, he'd say watch me. There just aren't enough adjectives that describe the kind of person he is. I thank God everyday that Joe is in my life. Not everyone can say that their brother is a superhero, but I can.

Love ya bro.

DJ Christensen
Joe's brother

***

Joe has impacted our lives in many ways over the past 8 or so years we have known him.

Our grandsons love coming to Florida and can't wait to go and see Joe and have a game of cards especially 99. Laughter always abounds.

No matter what kind of day you may be having you just have to look at Joes' smile and your day looks brighter.

Some may see Joe as having a disability or physically challenged but they just don't know him. There is nothing that he won't try ... can't is not in his vocabulary. When faced with a challenge or maybe a suggestion to try something Joe dives right in and always with a total commitment to his endeavour. We are always in awe as he keeps moving on to bigger and better projects. Failure is not an option he just keeps working through it.

To show this positive attitude has been amazing for us to witness and learn from. His eagerness to share his ideas is infectious you can't help but to be excited for him. Oh, did I mention he does love to talk!!

He will tell you about his health problems at birth and throughout the years like it is a story to be told. It is not a "poor me" story but just the facts! His ability to overcome these obstacles is awe inspiring.

It is our pleasure to know Joe and to watch just to see what he will think of next to do.

He is a friend to all he meets old and young and we are truly happy to be considered a friend to Joe and his family.

Sue & Derick Hamer
Family friends

***

Joey and I are cousins, born about six months apart. We grew up doing a lot of things kids do together. We would hang out at family cookouts and riding bikes or playing Spud!, go to each other's houses to play Sega or Nintendo for (probably too many) hours at a time, and we even went to Western Lanes every Saturday where we would compete on the same bowling team. To me, he was always just Joey; the guy who I liked to annoy by squeezing his knee; the guy who really didn't like it when you messed up his hair; the guy I would practice my sign language with.

It wasn't until much later that I realized Joey had a bigger impact on my life. I have grown to realize he taught me to never question someone's ability to accomplish their goals or achieve their dreams. Never once did I question if he could do something I was doing (and I don't recall a single time he questioned himself, either). In fact, he often challenged me to do better or try harder.

He taught me to greet everyone with my arms and

heart open. Joey was always happy, smiling from ear to ear. No matter where we went he seemed to make friends with whoever was nearby. Recently he stood up as a groomsman in my wedding. By the end of the night he had connected with all of the other groomsmen and even had them following him outside so he could get a picture with them all. He truly has a gift that allows him to connect with others.

He taught me to ask not "if" someone can do something but "how" they can do it. I currently work at a university with college students. Each day I find myself challenging my students to strive to be their best. When they feel deflated or are struggling with something we talk about how they can overcome their troubles, not if they can. Joey was never afraid to try something new. If he had trouble, he would find a way to make it work. He never gave up and never made excuses.

Having him in my life has given me the ability to see the potential each individual has and embrace the differences and experiences unique to us all. I hope to spread the impact Joey has had on my life by continuing to share these lessons with my students and everyone around me.

Love you!

Jess Simon
Joe's cousin

***

Twenty five years ago, I was working my first job as a sign language interpreter in a kindergarten classroom. Although it sounds cliché, I still remember my first day and the eight deaf and hard-of-hearing students with whom I worked. One of them stands out more so in my memory, however. He was a skinny, pale, fragile-looking boy with sunken eyes and arms and legs that seemed to hardly function. These weren't the traits that most intrigued me, though. I was most fascinated with the smile on his face, which I quickly learned over the next two years was a contagious quality. During that time he taught me not only the importance of a sunny disposition, but the power of perseverance. Even at the age of five, Joe was impacting those around him with a spirit like no other. I recall him as one of the hardest workers I'd ever seen. Physical barriers never got in the way of his effort and he rarely asked for assistance with tasks. His classmates never saw him as different. They just saw him as a friend.

Years passed and Joe left elementary school. As educators often do, I wondered whatever happened to my former student, such a frail little boy. I recalled reading in his file that his life expectancy was to be limited. Deep inside, I doubted if Joe was even on this earth anymore. Thankfully, I was wrong. Twenty years after I'd seen that smile for what I thought was the last time, it appeared on my social media feed.

I was thrilled to re-connect with Joe! Conversation with this now young man was just as upbeat and positive as it had been when he was a child. We both now shared a common interest in fitness, as I was beginning to delve into distance running and Joe was introduced to My Team Triumph. Joe told me about the program, which allowed people with various disabilities to participate in running events they couldn't physically accomplish alone. It was the perfect venue to re-connect and I was honored to be on Joe's team for his first ever race. The joy he experienced in this event was tenfold for me. Watching his face as we crossed that finish line instilled in me that perseverance is the key to success. Joe will not accept failure and defies opposition, despite any physical difficulty. It's a quality I try to model in my own life, too.

Just months after my first run with Team Joe, I completed my first full marathon. It was a struggle physically, mentally, and emotionally, but when things got tough I dedicated those miles to Joe. His lessons helped pull me through. Whatever hardships we encounter, I've seen the power of not giving up, and moreover doing so with a positive attitude.

Looking back, I realize that Joe and I have completely reversed our roles as student and teacher. Quite frankly, the lessons he has taught me far outweigh anything I could have taught him. I'm humbled to call him not only a teacher, but a role model, an inspiration, and mostly a friend.

Lisa Andreas
Joe's sign language interpreter

***

Joseph,

When I was asked to write a letter for your book, I thought it would be very simple, as words have always been easy for you and I. However, when I tried to put my thoughts down, it was more difficult than I expected.

Where do I begin?

How do I tell you that while you may be changing the world for so many these last several years, you have been changing our family for 31 years.

How do I tell you that you taught Britney and Zachary to never look at the differently-abled differently. For so long, when you were all young, they never knew that you had limits. I thank you for showing them to look at the soul of a person and not their physical being.

How do I tell you how much it means to see the amazing bond you and Grama share. It warms my heart to see you together.

How do I tell you that you are the most incredible Uncle I have ever seen; Kara, Logan and Ella are so lucky to have you in their lives.

How do I tell you that you and your mother have the purest of all mother/son loves, and it's a gift. You make each other better, stronger. Always, together.

How do I tell you that you are the strongest, most unselfish, loving person I have ever had the honor of knowing and loving.

How do I tell you the affect you have on those around you- how you give everyone hope. How you show that even if you are dealt a bad hand in life, you can still play it to win ~ and win BIG! Never once do you complain or ask "why me". You push and push yourself to keep giving good back in life.

How do I tell you that you are my Hero?

Each and every day I see things that could turn even those with the strongest faith bitter. I see you embrace each hurdle as a challenge to be won. I see you remain the sweet, silly, loving soul that you are. I see the physical struggles you endure, but always face them with that beautiful, courageous smile. I see a man that has touched every single person he has met along the way and brought them all some joy and hope. I see the person that I hope to be a little bit like someday. I see a gift that God has given to our family. I see you Joe.

How do I tell you everything that is in my heart? I guess I hope you already know.

I hope you know that I am the proudest I can ever be of you. I hope you know you bring me hope and love and happiness. I hope you know you have taught me that there is such pure goodness in this not so good world. I hope you know you are my Hero.

Love,

Doreen Koch
Joe's aunt

***

As a professional, I work as a sign language interpreter, I have met and worked with students of all abilities in my time in the schools. I met Joey several years ago when I was introduced to the organization My Team Triumph by a mutual friend and fellow interpreter. We joined Team Joey and got to be part of his first racing adventure at the Bellin Run! I had been a runner for about 10 years prior to meeting Joey and becoming involved with My Team Triumph, but running took on a whole new meaning for me after my experiences with Joey. I had always ran for time and would be disappointed in myself if I did not reach a goal or distance, I was getting burnt out! mTT was a breath of fresh air, a place where running was fun again and knowing that Joey was having a blast made every mile more enjoyable. When I lace up my shoes now, I do it to clear my head and to get stronger not only physically but mentally too. In my work, I am reminded by Joey and the mTT athletes and crew, that anything is possible if you want it bad enough. I am a better advocate for the students I work with and am dedicated to staying positive. Joey is always smiling and his attitude is one that everyone should emulate. This summer I will be running with Team Joey for the sixth time, and I am honored to have gotten to know him and be part of his inspiring journey.

Jericho Schneider
mTT Angel

***

There is a legend in the writing world that Ernest Hemingway was able to use only 6 words to write his story. Many teachers use this to inspire students to express an important story in their lives. I remember, it was last May, as the school year was wrapping up, my students were struggling with really finding something meaningful to say for their six word memoir and I went home and saw that Joe had posted this picture with a six word caption.

"Through friendship, all things are possible."

Through friendship, all things are possible. It's difficult to put into words the impact Joe has had on my life. His words describe it better than I ever could. But that's what Joe does, he believes all things are possible, for everyone. And that's why he puts it in words better than anyone else, because he knows that all things are possible. Joe brings his 10 mile-wide smile and positive attitude (and sometimes doughnuts) and shares it with everyone he comes in contact with and we are all better because of his influence in our lives.

Thank you, Joe

Amanda Lacey-Couch
mTT Angel

***

JC,

Are you as surprised as I am that our friendship is nearing 10 years already? Time flies! It's been rewarding getting to know you and what you've been through. Your story is truly remarkable. We've shared a lot of laughs over countless things, but I probably don't tell you often enough how much you inspire me.

Being down the road you've traveled hasn't been easy, yet your perseverance is extraordinary. In the face of adversity, you've overcome a myriad of obstacles. What's most impressive is that you've done it with such a positive attitude. Your outlook on life is filled with optimism. I've learned something from your glass half full mentality. It would be easy for you to show frustration with some of the things you've had to cope with, but you don't waste your time with that. You harness positive energy, focus on the good and accomplish impressive things.

Remarkably, you haven't stopped at living your own life to the fullest. You've become an advocate for the differently abled. Your story has enlightened so many people. It's a wonderful reminder that life can only limit you as much as you allow it to. I love seeing you celebrate your achievements because it encourages me to never give up. I ask myself, if JC can defy the odds and accomplish great things, why should I settle for good enough? I want to give every day 100% like you do *every single day*. You have no idea how powerful your message is to those around you.

Our friendship serves as a daily reminder to myself that I can overcome adversity. If I'm presented with a problem, the first question I ask myself shouldn't be "Why me?" – it needs to be "How can I conquer this?" – or more pointedly, "WWJCD?" That would also make for a more marketable bracelet. File that idea away for later.

No one could prouder of you than your friends and family for your work with myTEAM TRIUMPH. I'm thrilled that you've found something that gives you as much joy as mTT has. That's another illustration of how you're not content to simply tackle long races and enjoy the ride. You're inspiring those around you. You're proving to fellow captains that they, too, can achieve awe-inspiring feats. I'm not sure if your initial motivation for joining mTT was to fulfill your own goals, but you've ended up helping others realize theirs along the way.

I need to get to my point, JC. You're an incredible person. You may inexplicably be a fan of the 0-for-4 Buffalo Bills. You may be into some absolutely wretched music. *Toby Keith?* **Seriously?** You may be a complete jabroni.

But you're a terrific person and a true friend. You make me want to be better. You make me want to fight through adversity. From one jabroni to another, thank you for inspiring me.

Your bro,
Dukester

P.S. When are we getting wings again, JC? Are you too busy with book signings now?

Duke Thomas
~~Joe's~~ JC's friend

***

Dear Joe (aka Captain Pancakes),

I remember first hearing about you from DoDo, my good friend and your Aunt Doreen. She often talked about her nephew, who she referred to as her hero. I remember thinking "Joe sounds like a great guy, but why does she keep calling him her hero?" At the time, I knew you had gone through a lot in your young life, but I didn't know your whole story.

Then, I got to meet you and run with you as your angel in the Bellin, and I learned more about you. I learned who Joe really was. And I understood why DoDo calls you her hero. Joe, you have become my hero, too, because now I know what sets you apart from the rest of us. It's not the surgeries you went through. It's not your different abledness. It's not that you spent your first weeks of life in the NICU.

It's your positive attitude. Your smile. Your outlook. I discovered through you what it means to have joy, even when life isn't going my way. To count my blessings. To complain less. Smile more. Embrace life on life's terms. Invaluable lessons I may never have learned if I hadn't met you.

Joe, you like to tell people that you are "differently abled" - not "disabled". I love that. LOVE IT. You know why? Because it leaves room to include ALL of us - including me! We are all differently abled. And when we work together, and pool our abilities - nothing is impossible. It's like when we ran the Bellin. I gave you a chance to run, and you gave me a chance to grow. I latched on to your spirit and you carried ME across the finish line!

I'm so proud of you, Joe, not only for all you have accomplished (and that's a lot!) but for who you are and how you raise me up when I am with you. I am honored to know you and call you friend. I can't wait to read your book!

Love,

Sue Degroot
mTT Angel

***

Joe,

I remember first meeting you at John F. Kennedy Elementary School where I worked as a Noon-Hour Supervisor. You were this little boy in a wheelchair using sign language to speak at times. Despite these differences, you were always surrounded by many, many friends. I think what attracted all of us to you was your smile. You were always smiling and it was always genuine. That is what I remember the most about you – your smile.

As I reflect back on those years at Kennedy, I specifically remember one time when you gave us all a scare. It was during lunch and you had a seizure. I remember you being so white. The ambulance came and took you away. We were all scared because we cared for you so much. It was awesome seeing you back at school shortly thereafter…you never let an obstacle stand in your way.

When you left Kennedy, I lost touch with you. Then, just a few years ago, our paths crossed again. I was at the baseball diamonds in Pulaski watching my grandson play baseball and there you were – Joey Christensen. You know what I first saw? You guessed it – that smile. It's hard to believe you are a grown man, but the one thing that hasn't changed a bit, is your smile and the positive aura that surrounds you.

Joe – I want you to know how special you are. You are a true role model and I think it's wonderful how you share your story with kids today. In fact, my grandson had the opportunity to hear you speak. He remembers you talking about overcoming obstacles and the importance of never giving up. For example, he remembers you sharing how buttoning your shirt wasn't easy, but you learned how using only one hand. He learned an important lesson from you – never let anything stand in the way of your dreams. When there is a will, there is a way!

I remember when you got up out of your wheelchair and walked using a cane. You did something some never thought you would. You are a true inspiration. Through all of the adversity and challenges thrown your way, you are one of the most positive people I know. I'm smiling just thinking about this memory – see, your smile is contagious!

I want you to know the impact you've had on me. You have taught me life lessons. First, never judge a book by its cover. Every person on this earth is different – it's ok to be different. Second, never give up. When there is a will, there is a way. And finally, stay positive. Negativity doesn't do anyone any good – choose to find the good with whomever crosses your path or whatever is thrown your way.

I'm so proud of you and the person you have become. To be authoring your own book – wow! I'm truly blessed to call you my friend. Keep reaching for the stars Joe!

Sue Neville
Kennedy Elementary School

***

Joey,

You are one of the most inspiring, influential, and opti-mistic people that I am blessed to have known since el-ementary school. Since birth you have defied the odds and have never allowed yourself to fall victim to a diagnosis most view with limits. You live your life limitless. Born with a death sentence and fighting for survival as you con-tinued to thrive is why I believe you have an extraordinary destiny. A destiny to change a world filled with diversity; one person at a time.

You've taught me that adversity does not define us. How we overcome adversity does. You focus on your abilities, which is how you continue to overcome obstacles. With a positive mindset and a heart full of determination you set out to accomplish what some may see as impossible and triumph through. Each leap of faith you have taken has given me the courage to do the same.

Life is a gift. A gift you have never taken for granted. You take advantage of the life you were given by spreading an important message. Being differently abled has enabled you to be a voice for others and change the way people view and accept one another. People from all walks of life can learn something from you. I've seen the change in perspectives and the impact you have on how people view individuals whom are differently abled. You've taught me that learning about our differences is what gives us a better understanding of one another. And with a better understanding comes a better connection. We're all human, right?

I'm extremely blessed to have crossed paths with you in our Kennedy Elementary School days. I'm a better person because of you. Keep changing the world, my friend.

Sarah Derozier
Joe's friend

***

Tennyson said, "I am a part of all that I have met". I have a front row seat on Joey's life. I saw the love and devotion of his parents, his struggle to survive, and how he endured some of the complications of prematurity. Mother Teresa said, "out of suffering comes perseverance; out of perseverance, courage; out of courage, hope; and out of hope, love". Joey has embodied and lived by these virtues. He has dealt with his disabilities in a exemplary fashion. And he continues to teach others how to do so also. He told me recently, "I am not disabled, I am differently abled." My life is better for knowing Joey Christensen!

Dr. Winston
Joe's Neonatal Doctor

***

I met Joey and my mind immediately started racing. I was not sure what he was looking to do? He kept talking about telling his story and I kept thinking about overcoming a disability. I was not sure what was special or different about his story. I was not even close.

As I listened to Joey's story, I realized the simplicity of the story and yet the profound impact it could have on Pulaski students. Joey was just a kid growing up, a kid that had to climb mountains to get where he was going. He talked about his fears, his likes and dislikes, and the hurdles he had to cross both physically and ones placed in front of him by other people. Joe talked about highlights in his life and some of the very lowest points. On the surface, this was a nice story, but still not much different than the story of hundreds of other students that pass through the doors of Pulaski every day.

The difference in Joe's story came with seeing him, watching him tie his shoe, listening to the names of teachers and administrators that made a difference. When you see the twinkle in Joey's eyes, when you hear the optimism in his voice, you simply end up falling in love with him and his story. Joe jumped into the world and the world bit him. Joe bit back.

Joe realized that the words people often used to describe him were simply not accurate. Joe knew he was not disabled or handicapped. The word he chose was "differently-abled". Joe explains to his audience that he can do most everything anyone else can do but he may do it a bit differently. It may take a little longer, but he can "get er done". Joe found people that were positive and he hooked his sail to them.

Joey's story makes kids realize there are no excuses. Take the hand you are dealt and play it. Your life can be fun and exciting. Your life can be an adventure. Look for the good in people and in situations.

Mark Heck
Pulaski Public Schools

***

Dear Joey,

We are so proud of you! You have been inspiring us for many years and we are so excited that the world will finally be able to share in your amazing story. This book is such a wonderful tool for you to reach even more hearts and lift them in the same way you lift ours every day.

Throughout your life, you have always shown unbelievable selflessness and positivity. You continue to shine despite every challenge thrown your way. Your ability to not only keep a smile on your face but to give that smile to everyone around you is one of the greatest things about you. We hope today you take a moment to recognize just how much you have impacted the community and how many lives you have touched. You have motivated your teammates through My Team Triumph, expanded the minds of hundreds of children through your speeches, given hope to many through the scholarship you created, and so much more. Your dedication to not only raising awareness but changing the way the world views differently abled individuals radiates through everything you do.

The impact you've had on our lives is no exception. The strength and wisdom you display each day pushes us to try to reflect it. You have taught us that change starts with one person and there is no limit to how much impact one person can have. While you often call some of your goals and achievements small, we are here to tell you that they are not small at all. Every step you take and every skill you master is huge to every single person that knows you. Every accomplishment is an example of the courage you have and the abilities you continue to grow.

We are blessed to call you our family and cannot wait to see all of the lives your new book is going to impact. You are a remarkable person with a remarkable story; one we have been lucky to experience by your side and are excited to reflect on through your own narrative. Thank you for sharing your past with us; we can't wait to see what the future holds for you.

Love,

Jaimie and Will
Family friends

***

Joey Christensen is an awesome person. He is an inspiration too me and others. He deals each day with issues I cannot comprehend with dignity and compassion. He has a wonderful personality and great smile always. Love him so much. He makes me thankful and appreciative of how great life is. He's delightful in everything imaginable. So thankful too be his friend .

Sandy Schulz
Family friend

***

I can still remember well my mother and I watching Joe being born and then rushing to neonatal unit. Tons of thoughts going through our heads after 90 days of ups and downs. He had the strength and will to go on. Thru it all, Joey never complained or asked "why me?" He always had a positive attitude. It did take its toll on our families, but his strong demeanor carried on.

It's not surprising that he tries to give back with speeches and other events. I truly believe he knows that he was meant to educate others and give back to society. I could not be prouder or more grateful of what he has become. He has become ten times the man that I could ever be and I love him dearly.

Don Christensen
Joe's dad

***

Who is JC?
Legend has it that he was thrown out of Hell because Hell couldn't handle him.

To me, JC is that kid on the blue motorized scooter doing burnouts on the playground asphalt.

He's bending his fingers completely backwards and laughing as the other kids cringe with delight.

He's our buddy teaching us sign language so we can talk across the classroom without getting in trouble with the teacher.

And he never backs down from any challenge. Have you ever tried playing JC on N64? You won't win.

And though looks can be deceiving, he is the strongest person I have ever met.

Countless surgeries were only slight growing pains to JC.

And let's be honest, he barely breaks a sweat during a Blazin' Wings challenge.

You would think that the odds are stacked against JC, but he easily topples them with a swift 'People's Elbow' or 'Stone Cold Stunner', just ask the Grim Reaper, who has received one every March 4th for the last 31 years.

As he continues to defeat the expectations other have set in his way, we can learn from JC to embrace the differences that life brings to us.

JC is my idol.

JC is my friend.

JC is Joe Christensen.

With love,

Tyler Gajewski
Joe's friend

***

If I had to pick just 1 way getting to know Joey has impacted my life, I would have to say, he has impacted my heart the most. The love he shows for his life, his family and his friends comes straight from his heart. To see this come from this young man with all the struggles he has overcome, melts my heart. Joey brings warmth over my heart every single time I see him. His great smile and laugh brightens any room. His personality is contagious ... I sincerely enjoy every single minute I get to spend with Joey and his amazing family

Diane Ruechel
Family friend

***

Everyone at some point in their life should meet a person (or two or three) who inspires them to be a better person. A person who motivates and drives them to achieve their dreams; their big, audacious, the sky's the limit type dreams. This type of friend becomes a foundation in our lives. They become one of the most genuine people we know and our lives in turn become better because of their friendship.

Luckily for me, I met this person while working for an organization that promotes authentic relationships. Joey Christenson is one of the most selfless people I know. From his own personal drive to always be moving forward to his pure heart of gold that desires to take care of everyone he meets; I know, that my life is better because he is in it.

I can remember very vividly one of the first conversations that Joey and I had one on one. He spoke about his famous phrase, "differently abled". His heart literally glowed while he spoke about his desire to bring social change where all abilities are celebrated and encouraged. In a world where we all have the abilities to make an impact, Joey motivates everyone to use their God-given strengths for good. Instead of focusing on what we cannot do, he challenges us all to focus on what we can do!

I know that God put Joey in my life for a reason. Through his life story of triumph shared in this book to his consistent enthusiasm for life, he teaches me that there is always a reason to celebrate. Because of this and for so many reason, I am blessed and honored to call him my friend.

Diane Gaywont
mTT Angel

***

I love how my awesome uncle can do stuff with me. He is so special to me. My uncle can do lots of things, he can play games with me and he knows how to do sign language and so do I. It is fun to spend my time with my uncle. I love my uncle because he is the best uncle in the world. Not all uncles are like my uncle. My uncle is handy-capped, that's why I love my favorite uncle.

Ella Thomson
Joe's niece

***

There's not much to say about my brother Joey that

everyone doesn't know already! He's strong, optimistic, happy, and just a joy to be around! But that didn't mean I was about to stop being a big sister! I dressed him up. Painted his nails. We both played hooky from school to go sledding. (Mom totally busted us!) Used his wheelchair. I even made him my personal maid here and there. He always said..." God gave your legs!!" my response was "yes and God gave me a little brother!" I'm proud to call him my brother and my friend! It's amazing to be part of his journey.

I love you Joe!!

Melissa Christensen
Joe's sister

***

Joe,

So many people have written you wonderful letters and have said a lot of what I would say. But when I thought about what else I could say that they didn't, I thought about our relationship and all the fun we had. How we started most of our days with a phone call, (well, when you finally woke up that is) even when you were in Florida. How we ate lunches together so many days of the week or sit outside on a nice day when your mom cut the lawn. How you got me to unpack all the trophies so that you didn't have too. And mostly how proud I am of you. You have come so far from the hard start you had, and have accomplished so much. I love how you are always smiling and happy, you make me smile! You are my buddy and I love you Joe, (how could anyone not love you). You should be proud of your book but more so, you should be proud of the young man you are becoming! You bring joy to all who know you, and I am thankful you are my grandson. Love you Joe!

Gram

***

Long story short: Joe Christensen is my hero.

Joe is the toughest person I have ever met. What Joe has gone through is unthinkable and incredible. He would meet every obstacle head on-with a smile on his face. I often wondered how could someone who has gone through so much, be THAT happy.

So, when I have had a bad day, I sometimes think of Joe. The day brightens after that.

Joe is my inspiration, and I am so proud to know Joe Christensen.

Dave Labar
Family friend

***

Dear Joe,

Just want to tell you how special you are to us. For years, you have inspired me with your courage, your confidence, and your ability to achieve more than anyone we know. I have had the distinct pleasure of being friends with your family for many years, and though we may not see each other as much in person, I can honestly tell you that the times spent with you and your family still brings a smile to my face. Of course, your mom and I shared more than a few bottles of wine during those years! I felt like a part of your family. You then welcomes Lee into the family once I married him as well and he also is so impressed with what you have done and what you have accomplished in your life.

One of the very endearing memories I have is being able to give your mom a short reprieve during one of your many visits to the Children's Hospital in Milwaukee and I got to spend the night and really felt bonded to you as I watched you come home smiling in your multiple casts. Yet through it all, you always put your best foot forward, making everyone around you feel better rather than focusing on yourself.

You've grown from one loveable little boy, into a wonderful and successful young man, who is still very lovable! We are so proud of you as our friend!

Congratulations on the book!

Love always,

Kathy and Lee Anderson
Family friends | mTT donors

***

Joey,

I don't know how to say this, because I know everyone else says it, but its true. You are a miracle and a showstopper. You have put such a huge impact on my life. Words cannot even express what I feel. Joes is one of the most kind, humble and magnificent people you will ever meet. He pulls on heartstrings that you never knew were there. Joe is an amazing uncle, friend, son and human being. He is always there for you no matter what, and his life experience is remarkable. His smile and sense of humor always light up the room. I've known Joey my whole life. He's always been there for me through both ups and downs and will always hold a special place in my heart. I love supporting him through everything he does. His determination and agility to do whatever he puts his mind to is exhilarating.

These past few years, Joey has worked with my team and helped us triumph. I believe he is having one of the best years of his life, every time he goes to run. When I see him cross the finish line, it brings tears of joy to my eyes, just seeing how happy it makes him. Being with him is never a dull moment and inspires you to never doubt yourself. Joey is a true inspiration even though he has gone through many hardships.

I love you Joey; your book is amazing and I cannot wait to read it. You are one of the nicest Quarter and Pancake loving people I have ever met. Never stop believing, and always know you have our love.

Love,

Kara Thomson
Joe's niece

***

We all have some of those unforgettable people in our lives that you can remember exactly when and where you first met them. For me, one of those people is Joe Christensen.

It was my first job right out of college. Joe was the very first student I saw as an Occupational Therapist. I remember being so unsure of myself, not really knowing what to expect. I walked into the side doors at the Pulaski Community Middle School and there was Joe and his mother, Dee. I was not sure how it was that a seventh grader could set me at such ease, but his infectious smile calmed my nerves instantly. It was on that day, and for the next four years, that I was blessed to become part of Joe's journey.

As a therapist, it was such pleasure to work with Joe. He was that bright spot in my week, a person that you looked forward to seeing. No matter how hard I pushed him and his body, he never gave up. He would always give 100% effort and somehow managed to keep his positive attitude through it all, despite the pain, the sweat and the frustration. It was in those moments that I got a clear picture of Joe's character, and his will to succeed. It was those qualities that have shaped him into the man he is today.

As a friend, it has been amazing to watch Joe's upward trajectory to a greater purpose. I have him grow up from a shy, 13-year old boy into the inspirational man he has become. Joes journey has been a challenging one, but he is a fighter. By sharing his story, joe has become a champion for ability, inclusion, and advocacy. He has been given a voice of hope to those with different abilities. Joe is living proof that with strength of character, belief in oneself, and the willingness to give it your all, you can overcome any obstacle that comes against you.

Now 18 years later, it is that same ear to ear, infectious smile that continues to touch my life and the lives of so many other people. Thank you, Joe, for being such an inspiration to us all!

Lyn (Bryfczynski) Boughton
Joe's childhood therapist

***

My dearest Joe,

As you know, we've been friends since the first grade. What you don't know is that it was because of you that I wanted to learn sign language. There were so many wonderful people around me speaking a language that I didn't understand. In some small way, I suppose I felt like the "odd man out." Sure, with the help of interpreters, we could have conversations, but that's not a practical approach on the playground or at the bowling alley. If we were going to be friends – true friends – I needed to speak your language.

In addition to watching Mrs. Nelson and Miss Bartels in the front of the classroom, I joined Kennedy's sign language club. And although I didn't have the raw, natural talent that a Sarah Derozier or Stephanie Nelson had, I was determined to learn how to sign. To this day, I still know my alphabet and several other words and phrases. But I do need to brush up… I'm not sure that I learned how to say "jabroni" using my hands.

Our faith teaches us that one of the best forms of prayer is to live a life rooted in joy, mindful that each and every day is a gift. And if that's the standard, I struggle to think of a bigger Prayer Warrior than you, JC. It has been a tremendous gift, and a true blessing, to have been your friend for all of these years.

The surest way to show praise and honor to God is to show love and grace to others. Because I've had the opportunity to know you, I better understand what it means to worship Him.

Keep kicking ass for Christ!

All of my love, today and all days,
TJV

Travis Vanden Heuvel
Joe's friend

Miss Guyot's 1st Grade Class | Kennedy Elementary

Miss Guyot
Mrs. Nelson
Anna Agabekova
Lloyd Anderson
Melissa Barrette

Ernest Boucher
Joey Christensen
Andy Ciha
Amanda Destree
Dawn Grossman

Ben Gulbrand
Amy Harris
Emily Manbevers
Tim Nockerts
Eric Nooker

Casie Nuthals
Racquel Rockey
Aaryn Schuster
Katie Skarda

Mandy Srenaski
Norbet VandenBranden
Travis VandenHeuvel
Brian VanEyck

Sign Language Club | Grade 1

ROW 1: (L to R)   Stephanie Nelson, Casie Nuthals, Matthew Gerrits, Amy Harris   ROW 2: Cara VanCamp, Amanda Boehm, Amanda Destree, Eric Nooker, Travis Vanden Heuvel, Brittany Nelson, Kelly Weber   ROW 3: Miss Hedstrom (Advisor), Nathan Schriver, Sarah Derozier, Katie Graf, Jennifer Dohm, Racquel Rockey, Norbert VandenBranden, Miss Bartels (Advisor)